PRENTICE HALL

Language Teaching Methodology Series

Classroom Techniques and Resources
General Editor: Christopher N. Candlin

Getting Students to Talk

Other titles in this series include:

CANDLIN, Christopher and MURPHY, Dermot
Language learning tasks

ELLIS, Rod
Classroom second language development

ELLIS, Rod
Classroom language acquisition in context

FRANK, Christine and RINVOLUCRI, Mario
Grammar in action

KENNEDY, Chris
Language planning and English language teaching

KRASHEN, Stephen
Second language acquisition and second language learning

KRASHEN, Stephen
Principles and practice in second language acquisition

KRASHEN, Stephen
Language acquisition and language education

KRASHEN, Stephen and TERRELL, Tracy
The natural approach

MARTON, Waldemar
Methods in English language teaching: frameworks and options

McKAY, Sandra
Teaching grammar

NEWMARK, Peter
Approaches to translation

NUNAN, David
Understanding language classrooms

PECK, Antony
Language teachers at work

ROBINSON, Gail
Crosscultural understanding

STEMPLESKI, Susan and TOMALIN, Barry
Video in action

STEVICK, Earl
Success with foreign languages

SWALES, John
Episodes in ESP

TAYLOR, Linda
Teaching and learning vocabulary

WALLACE, Catherine
Learning to read in a multicultural society

WENDEN, Anita and RUBIN, Joan
Learner strategies in language learning

YALDEN, Janice
The communicative syllabus

Getting Students to Talk

A Resource Book for Teachers
with Role-Plays, Simulations and Discussions

Aleksandra Gołębiowska

Edited and Adapted by Jim Wingate

ENGLISH LANGUAGE TEACHING

Prentice Hall

New York London Toronto Sydney Tokyo

First published 1987 as *Let's Talk: A Book for Teachers*
by Wydawnictwa Szkolne i Pedagogiczne
This edition first published 1990 by
Prentice Hall International (UK) Ltd
66 Wood Lane End, Hemel Hempstead
Hertfordshire HP2 4RG
A division of
Simon & Schuster International Group

© Prentice Hall International (UK) Ltd, 1990

Typeset in 10 pt Times
by MHL Typesetting Ltd, Coventry

Printed and bound in Great Britain at the
University Press, Cambridge

Library of Congress Cataloging-in-Publication Data

Gołębiowska, Aleksandra.
    Getting students to talk / by Aleksandra Gołębiowska : edited and
adapted by Jim Wingate.
        p.   cm. — (Language teaching methodology series)
    'A resource book for teachers with role-plays, simulations, and
discussions' —
    Rev. ed. of: Let's talk. 1987.
    ISBN 0—13—355090—7 $9.00
    1. English language — Study and teaching — Foreign speakers.
2. English language — Spoken English. 3. Discussion. I. Wingate.
Jim. II. Gołębiowska, Aleksandra. Let's talk. III. Title.
IV. Series.
PE1128.A2G64   1990
428.007 — dc20   89—29166
                                                            CIP

British Library Cataloguing in Publication Data

Gołębiowska, Aleksandra
    Getting students to talk : resource book for teachers with
    role-plays, simulations and discussions. — (Language
    teaching methodology series).
    1. Spoken English language
    I: Title   II. Gołębiowska, Aleksandra. Let's talk   III.
    Wingate, Jim   IV. Series
    428.3

    ISBN 0—13—355090—7

---

1 2 3 4 5   94 93 92 91 90

Contents

* The language of discussion

General Editor's Preface

At the risk of stating the obvious, 'Getting students to talk' is the major and one of the most difficult tasks confronting any teacher of languages. But talk they must; not only because research into second language acquisition consistently advocates developing a context of spoken interaction in the classroom as the key variable in the quality and the quantity of student language learning, but also because it is through cooperative talking that learners are enabled to simulate and thus prepare for the actuality of out-of-class communication.

Talking is thus not only one of the intended outcomes of classroom instruction but also the means by which other objectives are addressed. Moreover, classroom talking is constrained by two important aspects of authenticity — that of goal and that of task. By authenticity of goal we refer to matching the conditions of the world beyond the classroom, while by authenticity of task we mean simulating in the classroom the essential conditions of talk, namely its purposefulness and its cooperativeness. Each of these constraints imposes major demands on the creativity and the classroom management skills of the teacher, especially in the normal conditions of much classroom language teaching, with large classes, learners of mixed ability and motivation and evaluated through forms of assessment in which talking may play a relatively limited and even minor role. We cannot overlook either the traditional patterns of teacher and learner role where cooperative talking is seen as an abnormality or where open-ended and divergent oral communication is seen as a subversion of the main agenda of the curriculum.

Encouraging talking, therefore, is much more than a matter of creating a lively classroom atmosphere, desirable though that is. Talk, as opposed to mere speech, has learning, teaching and evaluating implications and, as a consequence, needs careful and well-motivated treatment.

Aleksandra Gołębiowska's new book in the Language Teaching Methodology Series tackles each of these issues. At one important level it is a resource book for the communicative classroom, full of ideas and techniques for enabling greater and more fluent spoken communication in the classroom. The wealth of techniques and task-types, all carefully organised and made accessible to the reader, pay tribute to this objective. At another level, however, it is a tool for action research in the classroom, a means by which the teacher can experiment with different types of task to assess variable outcomes, both in terms of types of talk and in terms of modes of learner participation. In this role, the book has much to offer the second-language acquisition researcher seeking ways to explore the effect of varied oral tasks on learner language acquisition. From yet another perspective, the book presents to teachers a convenient and immediately useful overview of the discoursal organisation of spoken contemporary English, a pedagogic discourse, if you like, as an adjunct to the grammars and the phonetics handbooks most teachers routinely possess. Part Three of the book addresses this role more directly.

I remarked earlier on the ease of access offered by the book. This is one of its most important attributes and one very much in keeping with sub-series C of the Language Teaching Methodology Series, that sub-series devoted to classroom techniques and resources. Not that Aleksandra's book is some disembodied and inhuman set of well-marshalled routines; it is characterised by a lightness and imagination, underpinned by solid conceptualisation at once typically Polish and also the hallmark of all good language teaching. In this treasure-trove every reader will find his or her favourite task. Mine must be No. 10 in the role-plays of Part Two (no prizes for guessing why!).

Finally, a word of great thanks to Jim Wingate who has adapted the book for a more international audience, but, I almost hasten to say, an audience seen through a pilgrim's eye, which makes all the difference.

Professor Christopher N. Candlin, *General Editor*
National Centre for English Language Teaching & Research
Macquarie University, Sydney

Preface

Getting Students to Talk is a resource book for those teachers of English who want to give their learners practice in oral communication. Since in real life speaking is frequently connected with other skills, many activities in this book involve both speaking and writing.

Getting Students to Talk has been written with the adult learner in mind, but many activities can be used with adolescents. The teacher will be the best judge of what will appeal to her learners. The appropriate levels are intermediate and upwards.

To make *Getting Students to Talk* as easy to use as possible

- the number of participants in most activities is flexible;
- alternative procedures are suggested;
- activities are followed by examples of the language that the learners might need, as well as by examples of typical mistakes;
- each activity is self-contained, although cross-references have been provided to enable the teacher to develop the activities according to the needs of her class;
- in the indexes at the back of the book, all the activities have been listed according to the number of participants that can take part in them, as well as to the subject-matter they touch on.

In order to take full advantage of *Getting Students to Talk*, it would be most advisable for teachers to read Part One first, as this explains how to use the role-plays most effectively. This part of the book will also make clear why *Getting Students to Talk* is not a teach-yourself book (except, perhaps, for Part Three) and why it cannot be used in those situations where there is one teacher to each learner. Moreover, *Getting Students to Talk* cannot be taken straight into the classroom. In the case of practically all the activities, some materials have to be duplicated and this cannot be avoided by asking the learners to buy the book.

Part One explains the rationale. Part Two contains all the role-plays, simulations and discussions, and the materials to duplicate. Part Three lays out all the language needed as functions. If you feel that your own English could be improved, check you are familiar with all the expressions in Part Three.

I hope that teachers will find *Getting Students to Talk* inspiring and stimulating.

Note: Throughout this book we use the convention that 'she' refers to the teacher, and 'he' to the learner. This does not undervalue male teachers or female students, but is simply for ease of reading.

Acknowledgement

I would like to express my sincere thanks to the three people who helped me write *Let's Talk*, the original title of *Getting Students To Talk*: my sister, Lucyna, who inspired me to write the book in the first place, Jan Rusiecki and Alec Bessey. All of them helped me enormously by reading the drafts, commenting on them and — last but not least — by boosting my confidence when inspiration was lacking.

Part One

How to Use
the Material

TEACHING TO COMMUNICATE

The aim of teaching English should be to enable our learners to communicate in that language. In order to achieve that aim, first we have to establish whom they will be communicating with.

In traditional classes the learners communicate mostly with their teacher only and, occasionally, with some other learners (see *The Role of the Teacher* later in this section). In either case, learners practise English first in the classroom and only later — if circumstances permit — outside the classroom, in real-life situations.

It is very important to prepare learners for the unpredictability of real communication, which is quite different from what can be found in pocket phrase-books. Unfortunately, making learners communicate with one another in something that resembles a real situation — the first step on the road to successful communicatioin — is quite a task. Creating situations in which the use of a foreign language is justified is one of the most untractable problems of foreign language teaching wherever the teacher shares the native language with her learners.

Communicating about classroom routine

Even though one may claim that any case of two or more native speakers of one language using a different language to communicate with one another is necessarily artificial, talking about homework, apologising for being late for a lesson, etc. is essentially different from discussing the problem of pollution, for instance. There is an element of naturalness in using English to communicate about the classroom routine of the English lessons.

Communicating about classroom routine is

- spontaneous;
- quite simple from the point of view of the language it involves and fairly predictable — it can therefore be easily taught and learnt and later provide a sense of achievement, particularly for the less successful learners;
- easy to accept because it is indispensable and well known from lessons of other subjects.

Examples are: 'I'm sorry I'm late', 'I've done my homework but . . .', 'Have you finished?', 'It's your turn now', 'I don't understand', 'What do I do next?', 'Is this right?',

1

'What does . . . mean?' The teacher can teach these and other examples early on, when the need arises, having used these expressions herself in previous lessons.

The above comments show that the teacher should not overlook the genuine — even if linguistically and communicatively limited — opportunities offered by the consistent use of English as the language of classroom management.

Pretending to be unable to speak the native language

As has already been pointed out, simulating situations in a foreign language is always artificial. That is why in some role-plays in this book only a few learners need pretend not to speak their native language. Still, somebody will have to pretend to be a foreigner (not necessarily a native speaker of English). Although for that one learner the role-play will be somewhat artificial, the others will thereby be justified in speaking English.

Foreigners may ask the way, need help in buying things or in ordering food in a restaurant, for example, but where else is English likely to be used?

Authentic local material

One way of finding out where English is needed is to have a look at a record of everyday life, i.e. your local or national newspapers, which are an inexhaustible source not only of authentic *materials* but also of authentic *situations*. In what kind of small ads is English mentioned or perhaps implied? Mostly in job advertisements. Practically everybody over sixteen is concerned about employment and/or money. Who is likely to need English in their job? A waiter in a holiday resort, a receptionist or telephonist in an international students' hostel, a mother's help for ambitious parents who would like their child to speak English. These are only a few examples of the temporary jobs that anyone, but particularly younger people, might be tempted to consider.

Other advertisements in which foreigners, and thus a foreign language, are mentioned or implied are the ones that concern accommodation. Having a flat to let is not as common as looking for a job, but even if a learner does not have one, he might be asked to interpret for somebody who does.

For international use the newspaper material presented here is from the English press, but you are encouraged to use your own papers which, though they are not in English, refer to authentic local jobs and accommodation. Ideal are English language papers published in some non-English-speaking countries. Such ads are doubly authentic: they refer to local situations and are in English.

The decision to base a fair number of activities on classified advertisements means that the scope of subjects and situations exploited is limited; but then it would be practically impossible to find a wide range of subjects and situations guaranteed to interest *everybody*.

Home-made role-plays

Those teachers who find that they are not happy with the choice of subjects and situations presented here should not reject the whole book, as they are wholeheartedly encouraged to extract the principles and techniques from *Getting Students to Talk* and proceed to create role-plays and simulations of their own. This encouragement also applies to those who accept the activities as they are. They too should try to write their own role-plays, as any materials created with a very clearly specified audience in mind — our own learners! — will be more appropriate than those produced for the international commercial market (see *Home-made Activities* in Part One).

Reality and motivation

Some of the comments made above touch on the problem of how real the situations exploited are. Undoubtedly, several simulations in *Getting Students to Talk* are not like real life at all (e.g. *Are You Honest?*). However, they do generate a great deal of discussion, which after all is the prime objective of this book.

It is extremely important always to bear in mind the overall aim of the book, i.e. inducing the learners to *talk*. Sometimes, learners are disappointed to find that there is no correct solution to the problem (e.g. in *Joanna*) or they dismiss the activities altogether as absurd and irrelevant. This difficulty may be solved by explaining quite explicitly that it is not the problem itself that matters as much as the process of arriving at its solution, which will invariably involve communicating in English.

Another way of dealing with those learners who would prefer a set solution is to point out that open-ended activities, i.e. activities in which they themselves have a definite influence on what is happening, are bound to be more challenging and stimulating.

ROLE-PLAYS, SIMULATIONS AND DISCUSSIONS

The activities in *Getting Students to Talk* can be divided into several types. The following table illustrates one of the possible classifications:

	The learner is told *who* he/she is	The learner is told *what* his/her views are	Example
1.	+	+	*Smoke*
2.	+	−	*Agony Aunt (1)*
3.	−	+	*Agree!*
4.	−	−	*Joanna*

The difference between the four types of activities may seem somewhat elusive but it can be summarised as follows: in types 1 and 2 the learner is assigned a specific role, while in types 3 and 4 he is not; in types 1 and 3 he is told what to say, in types 2 and 4 he is not.

If you like, in *Joanna* each learner is entirely himself, in *Smoking* each learner is entirely the role given, whereas in *Agony Aunt* each learner becomes a different person, yet expresses his own opinions, and in *Agree!* each learner is himself, yet is given views to express which are not necessarily his own. Any role-play, simulation or discussion can be classified as one of these four types.

Information gap, opinion gap

Real-life communication is usually stimulated by the fact that people either know different things or have different opinions. If communicative activities are to resemble real-life communication — which is certainly their aim — can it be assumed that learners will have different opinions on a given subject? If the problem under discussion is sufficiently complicated and controversial, it would be an extraordinary coincidence if everybody had exactly the same views. In other cases, however, it is safer to assign divergent opinions. It is also possible to let the learners have different pieces of information regarding the situation in question.

Thus the ambitious aim of imitating real-life communication is best achieved by having disagreement built into the communicative activities. The learners talk because some of them know something *the others do not know* (e.g. in *The Once-in-a-Lifetime Holiday*, Mr and Mrs Notkin *do not know* that Baker and Smith are fraudsters), or because they have conflicting views (e.g. in *Expectations* the Boltons and the Jenkinses have different opinions about the baby's future). The participants' opinions can also be different because they know different things (e.g. in *The Flat* Marianne is the only person who is definitely against renting out the flat, but nobody else knows about her wedding plans). In order to make an activity more challenging, learners can be given a piece of information with the stipulation that it is not to be disclosed, although it has to be acted upon (e.g. in *Bread*, Father cannot disclose the real reason for not wanting to go to the bakery).

Awareness of the information gap concept can result in yet another classification of communicative activities, namely into those with an information gap and those without.

A helpful, simple definition is that role-play has an information gap, and simulation and discussion have an opinion gap.

Two features occur again and again in the design of the most successful communication games, and both depend on there being some built-in disparity between players during the game, which takes its impetus from the players' attempts to close this gap or overcome this difference. For the first feature I borrow the term 'information gap'; for the second 'opinion gap' seems a reasonable label. By information gap I mean that players start the game with different amounts of information. In order to play the game they need to communicate the missing pieces of information to one another. . . . Because of this need to share information, games of this type are most often cooperative, with the group as a whole trying, so to speak, to 'beat the system'. The second procedure is more suited to competitive games, since it trades on that facet of human nature that enjoys winning an advantage by clever manipulation of facts. The 'gap' consists in the other player's tendency to disagree with anything that helps an opponent. (Rixon 1979: 104, 105)

A close analysis of the role-plays in this book will show that maintaining the information gap is crucial if this type of activity is to be successful. What this means in practical terms is that *on no condition should learners look at one another's role-cards*. As this is an essential factor in all role-plays, it might be advisable to make learners explicitly aware of the importance of this rule (see *Rules* later in this section).

In simulations and discussions one need not worry about maintaining the information gap, as there is none. The success of those activities is guaranteed by the task the learners are presented with, the task which, in turn, guarantees a wide range of opinions, i.e. secures the opinion gap.

Simulations and discussions

The difference between simulations and discussions is simple.

In simulations the learners are assigned roles that justify their communication. They may be told to imagine they are members of a committee and have to decide on something. This may mean choosing the best competition entry (in *Pet Hate*) or deciding who should adopt a baby (in *Baby Girl for Adoption*). The learners may be told they are employees of a company and have to plan an advertising campaign (in *An Ad Campaign*) or that they work for a magazine and are faced with the task of answering a difficult letter (in *Agony Aunt (1)*).

Discussions are more traditional. The learners are presented with a problem and have to express their opinions about it. The few discussions in *Getting Students to Talk* have been made more appealing to the learner, for instance, by stipulating reaching a unanimous decision (in *Robert Slater*), or telling the learners to argue for a certain point of view even if contrary to their personal convictions (in *Agree!*). The latter technique of making learners argue against their own views is a very useful one since it helps them realise how many aspects every problem has. This technique can also be used with some simulations (*Baby Girl for Adoption, Are You Honest?*).

To sum up:

A *role-play* is a communicative activity in which the learners are given a task to complete. In order to ensure a lively and unpredictable course of the activity, the learners are told who they are, what their opinions are and what they know that is unknown to the others.

A *simulation* is a communicative activity in which learners are told who they are and what their task is. They present arguments according to their *own* beliefs.

A *discussion* is a communicative activity in which learners retain their own personalities and views. Their task is to come to an agreement regarding an issue introduced by the teacher.

It is difficult to predict if a particular group of learners will have a preference for one type of communicative activity over the other two. A lot of teachers agree though that young people who have only just stepped into adulthood often dislike hiding behind roles; they are proud of their own minds and want to express their views wherever and whenever they can. They thus prefer the simulations and discussions to the role-plays unless the roles given closely resemble their own reality. On the other hand, if they know that role-plays usually lead to discussions on the issues of the role-plays they are happy to have a role-play as a rehearsal of the language given to express their own opinions later.

GROUP WORK

Group work is an inherent part of any effective lesson because

- it generates more student talking time than any other technique;
- it frees the teacher to teach more effectively (see *The Role of the Teacher* later in this section);
- it is learner-centred and thus actively involves all learners;
- it makes learners responsible for their own learning;
- it is beneficial to the development of group dynamics.

It is up to individual teachers to decide whether groups should have leaders. The decision, however, should depend on what their function is to be. If they are to make sure that everybody speaks English, that none of the material is lost and that, generally speaking, everything runs smoothly then by all means the teacher should let each group of learners choose their leader. (Appointing one would be a case of unnecessary teacher intervention.)

The teacher must also decide whether or not to set up groups in which the English of all the learners is approximately at the same level. Adopting this style means that weak learners will not be inhibited by the more advanced ones and that the advanced learners will not be held back by the weaker ones. On the other hand, students learn as much from one another as from the teacher and so less experienced learners grouped together are likely to progress at a slower rate with fewer examples in sight to follow. Also with mixed-level groups the more proficient learners can make sure that an activity is progressing well, so the responsibility for the success of the lesson does not rest with the teacher alone.

> Some teaching authorities, for instance F.L. Billows (1961), have argued that one of the teacher's main functions is to design the kinds of activities that will encourage students to learn from each other and therefore be less dependent on the teacher (McDonough 1981: 84—5).

From a practical point of view, therefore, setting up mixed-ability groups is simpler and the groups thus formed are more likely to be based on the principles of friendliness, which is much safer than teacher intervention.

SIZE OF GROUPS

Most of the activities in this book are flexible enough for the teacher not to worry about an inconvenient number of learners ('I have a role-play for six groups of four. What should I do if nineteen pupils are present tomorrow?'). In many cases there are optional roles, which can be omitted if there are too few learners (e.g. Paula's godfather in *Jam*). If there are more participants than roles, the teacher can draw on the emergency cards that are suitable for practically all role-plays (see *Emergency Role-Cards* later in this section). If the same role-play is going on simultaneously in various groups, it is not necessary for all groups to be of the same size (e.g. in *Bread* there can be three groups consisting of four students — Mother, Father, Daughter and Son — and two groups of three students — Mother, Father and Daughter only). Thirty learners can be divided into six groups of four and two groups of three; fifteen learners into three groups of four and one group of three, etc.

The above comments do not apply to simulations, since the number of participants there is not strictly specified. The teacher should remember, however, that the smaller each group in a class, the more effective the activity will be. No matter how well designed a communicative activity is, if there are too many students in each group, there is a chance that at least one participant will assume the role of a 'passenger' who lets the others do all the work.

EMERGENCY ROLE-CARDS

The following role-cards can be used whenever there are more learners than parts in a role-play, e.g. four people in one group for a three-person role-play.

> You are not quite sure what the whole conversation is about but you like the sound of your own voice.

> You cannot make up your mind. First your support one side, then another/the other.

> Choose a point of view you agree with and which has been expressed by somebody else. Keep suggesting the same idea, but put it in different words. You don't want to admit that you subscribe to somebody else's views.

It sometimes happens that for one reason or another, a learner cannot fully participate in an activity, e.g. he joined the class in the middle of the term and needs to be allowed some time to adapt. In such cases the teacher may decide to give that learner a less demanding card.

> Contradict everything the person on your left says.

> Confirm everything the person on your right says.

> You think the person on your left/right speaks too loudly. Without asking explicitly (you are shy), try to make that person speak more softly.

THE PHYSICAL LAYOUT OF THE CLASSROOM

During communicative activities it is best to push desks back and arrange the chairs into circles of appropriate size.

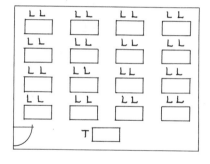

Here is a classroom with thirty-two learners (LL) sitting at desks and the teacher (T) at the front.

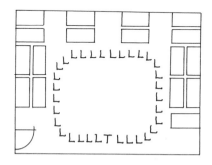

Here is the same classroom after two minutes of moving chairs and desks. The learners (LL) are sitting in a tight circle with the teacher. The tables can be moved back again in two minutes at the end of the lesson to minimise noise disturbance to neighbouring rooms.

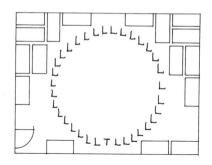

Here is the same classroom with a further minute of moving tables so that the learners form a much larger circle. The tables can be rearranged in three minutes at the end of the lesson to minimise noise disturbance to other rooms.

The teacher can draw the diagram of the desired room arrangement on a large sheet of paper and the very *first* thing the learners do at or before the beginning of the lesson is to arrange the room as the diagram shows so the rooms next door or below are not disturbed. The learners soon become more proficient, quicker and quieter at moving furniture.

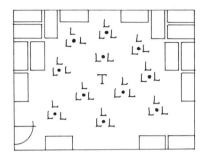

Here is the same classroom with the learners sitting doing role-plays in threes. There is one group of two because there are thirty-two in this class. Those two learners could equally well each add themselves to a three to make two fours. The teacher (T) is free to circulate, checking, encouraging and helping. The dots are the focal points of each group.

If we look down on a learner from above we see or . If we look down

on a teacher from above we see .

Here are suggestions for making pairs, threes, fours, fives and sixes for a classroom with fixed furniture.

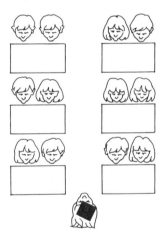

ones

Here is *a section of the classroom* with twelve learners sitting in pairs at six desks. You can see by the way their chins are pointing that they are all looking to the front, e.g. at the teacher, so that the teacher does all the work.

twos

Here are the same twelve learners doing pair work with the teacher listening. The dots show where each pair is focusing.

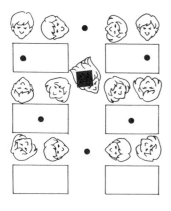

twos

Here are the same twelve learners doing pair work, but pairing with a new partner this time, although they are each sitting in their original places. The teacher is helping.

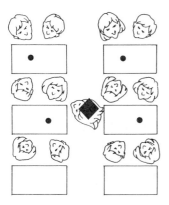

threes

Here are the same twelve learners working in threes. They still have not changed seats. The teacher is listening to one group of three.

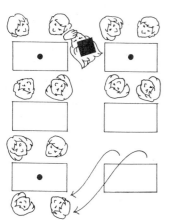

fours

Here are the same twelve learners working in fours. Only two of the learners have had to move. The teacher is whispering a word (vocabulary item?) to one of the learners.

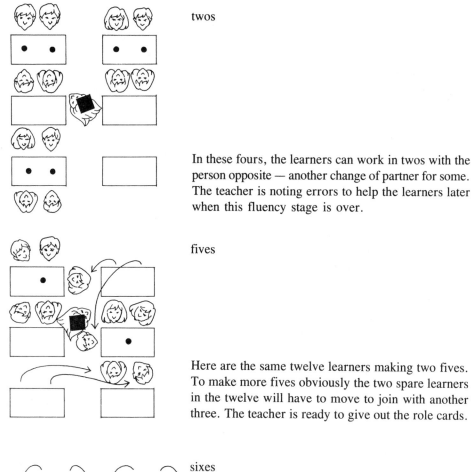

twos

In these fours, the learners can work in twos with the person opposite — another change of partner for some. The teacher is noting errors to help the learners later when this fluency stage is over.

fives

Here are the same twelve learners making two fives. To make more fives obviously the two spare learners in the twelve will have to move to join with another three. The teacher is ready to give out the role cards.

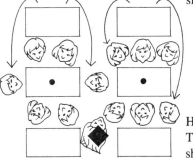

sixes

Here are the same twelve learners making two sixes. The teacher is noting a few words they are using which she didn't know they knew.

Try drawing your classroom(s) and see how you could move the furniture and/or the learners to help group work.

RULES

Practice has shown that before learners become fully acquainted with communicative activities in general and role-plays in particular they tend to forget certain basic principles. The result is that the activity fails and the learners, together with their teacher, lose heart. That is why it is advisable to let the learners have these three rules in front of them at all times:

Don't Show Your Role-card to Anyone
Don't Reveal all the Information at Once
Speak English

The most effective way of making the learners remember the three imperatives is to *write them on all role-cards*. In this way, whenever the learners consult their card they are reminded of the principles. It should be noted here that writing the rules on the blackboard, although much less trouble, is inadvisable, since, the learners are not very likely to look at the blackboard while engaged in what they are doing, especially if their backs are to the board.

The teacher may decide to prepare rule-sheets and distribute them among the class, one per group. The more attractive and eye-catching they are, the more likely they are to be effective, e.g. with drawings or coloured inks, or written over attractive pictures glued onto card.

MATERIALS

After a close reading of *Getting Students to Talk* it soon becomes obvious that the teacher has quite a lot of copying to do before she can take the activities into the classroom. She should by no means be deterred by the fact, since once the materials are prepared they can be used over and over again. For this reason, it is worthwhile preparing the materials carefully, with every effort to make them both attractive and durable.

Here is a list of the types of material the teacher might have to prepare:

● **name-cards** (as on international conference tables) for those role-plays where there are more than two characters and where they have names given (e.g. in *The Neighbours*). Those name-cards will help learners remember who is who in the role-play and by what names they should address one another;

- **role-cards**, i.e. information known to individual participants only. Even if some — or all — of the items on the role-cards are identical (e.g. in *Barbara and Anna*) the learners should not be made aware of that fact. Role-cards are necessary for all role-plays;

- **background information**, i.e. information known to all the participants. It is necessary for some role-plays (e.g. news of Mrs Bennett's impending contract in *The Flat*) and for all simulations;
- **rule-sheets**, unless the rules are copied onto the role-cards (see *Rules*).

They are necessary for all role-plays.

All the materials will last longer if they are made of card and are stored carefully. If the role-cards, rule-sheets, etc. are the size of a postcard they can be conveniently stored in envelopes.

So, the motto is 'Be prepared'.

...The most common causes of potential chaos ...
The materials look too childish or boring.
The materials are too complicated.
There are not enough materials to go round the groups or pairs.
The materials used are not complete, e.g. pieces missing from sets of games.
The materials are in the wrong order. (Willis 1983: 32).

PROCEDURE — PREPARE THE IDEAS FIRST

Learners will benefit most from communicative activities if they are adequately prepared to take part in them. They are given the new items before they need them, so that when the need arises (i.e. in the activity) they are already equipped to cope.

The teacher may first wish to introduce the general theme of the role-play (e.g. in the case of *The Neighbours* the advantages and disadvantages of living in a block of flats). She has to be careful, though, not to spend *too* much time on this preliminary discussion of the theme, so that the subject is not exhausted before the role-play takes place.

For a teacher of English, the language used in a discussion is perhaps more important than the subject-matter. In fact, all the activities in this book are basically a device to make learners talk. That is why it is necessary to devote some time to the language those activities generate. Since they are aimed at intermediate and advanced learners, there should not be too many problems with pronunciation, vocabulary or grammar. Experience has shown, however, that even advanced learners are often unable to vary the way of expressing the same meaning. That is why those functions that are most likely to be of use in a role-play or simulation are also listed in Part Three.

When the teacher is preparing a lesson she may decide to take the usual approach and plan to elicit or pre-teach the functions that the learners will need during the subsequent activity. This can be done in the same way that one elicits or pre-teaches language during any other lesson.

When the time for the actual role-play comes, the learners should always be given time to read their role-cards and prepare an outline of what they are going to say.

It is possible, for variety's sake, to ask all the learners assigned the same role to work together at this stage. After the learners have discussed their parts, they then regroup to take part in the role-play proper.

Worked example of 'Can You Cook?' role-play

There are three characters in this role-play — Teresa (A), Mr McDonald (B) and Mrs McDonald (C). With a class of twelve, there are four groups of three learners.

Allocating roles

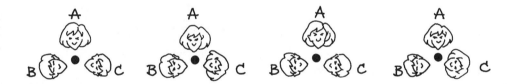

Suitable learners in each group are allocated roles. The teacher decides who is going to play which character in the role-play. This can be done in a number of ways. The teacher can allocate roles according to the student's language proficiency or personality, or at random. It is up to the individual teacher to decide which criterion she is going to use. It is necessary, however, to point out the dangers of 'type-casting'. Learners classified as poor, shy or unimaginative might have difficulty showing that they have changed or that they were incorrectly labelled in the first place.

After the learners have been allocated the roles, all the A's (i.e. all the students role-playing Teresa) get together to prepare being that character. All the B's (Mr McDonald) get together at the same time, as do all the C's (Mrs McDonald). With twelve students this makes groups of four of each character.

Reading the role-cards and preparation

Having prepared, they then re-form their original threes to do the role-play.

Doing the role-play

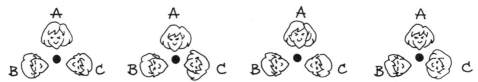

The above arrangement will encourage the learners to discuss among themselves any doubts they have, without referring straightaway to the teacher. In this way they learn to be more independent. They can also exchange their views as to the interpretation of the role-cards and compare their guesses as to how the role-play will develop (e.g. in *Can You Cook?* those learners who have the part of Teresa may try to predict what questions they will be asked). This stage of the lesson can also be a substitute for the introduction of the general theme by the teacher, discussed earlier in this section.

Alternative procedure — First create the need for the language

It was pointed out above that the usual procedure of dealing with the functions that learners will need during a role-play is to practise them before the role-play starts. There is an alternative procedure, which is particularly applicable in those situations in which the teacher plans two similar role-plays to follow each other closely. In those cases it is possible to work on the new language *after* the first activity. The teacher then points out to the learners that there are certain phrases, functions, etc. that they could have used to convey their message more adequately. The learners then have a chance to use those new expressions, etc. in the second version of the role-play. The first role-play creates a need for the new expressions, then the second one satisfies that need.

One of the reasons why it is worthwhile to conduct a role-play twice is that the learner is given a chance to improve on the first performance without knowing exactly how the situation will develop (as would be the case if role-plays were exactly the same).

Another reason for doing a role-play twice is that while a role-play is in progress learners often think: 'If I were her, I'd deal with the problem in a different way'. Conducting the same role-play again, with learners allotted different roles, provides the learners with an opportunity to work things out in a different way, with the benefit of hindsight. In this case the fact that there is no information gap should not be a deterrent. The opinion gap will not be affected, of course.

Procedure for simulations

The procedure for using simulations differs somewhat from that described above for role-plays.

Simulations are based on the principle of the opinion gap. Once a problem has been discussed, there is no reason to come back to it, and so there is no point in staging the same simulation twice. It follows then that the discussion of the language material cannot be left until after the activity. This does not imply that simulations — or discussions, for that matter — need to be routine.

One way of enhancing those activities which require arranging some elements or facts in a predetermined order is to use the pyramid discussion format.

Worked example (sixteen students in the class)

Let us use *Are You Honest?* as an example:

Pyramid discussion format

Students as individuals each look at ten cases of dishonest acts described in a list. Each student evaluates each of the cases giving each one a score of between 1 and 10 (completely honest 1, utterly dishonest 10).

Here is a class of sixteen students working individually. (We represent them in a line for the convenience of the diagram only.)

Stage one

When each learner has finished his evaluation, all the learners make pairs and compare their evaluations. The task for each pair is to agree a single evaluation between them.

Stage two

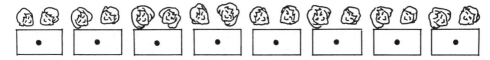

After that negotiation, pairs get together into fours and again compare, discuss and negotiate to agree a single evaluation between all four.

Stage three

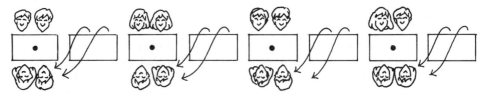

After that negotiation, fours get together into eights and again compare, discuss and negotiate to agree a single evaluation between all eight.

Stage four

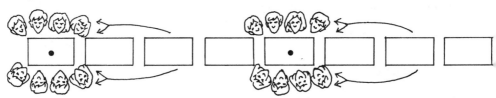

After that the eights get together into a sixteen, again to arrive at a single agreed evaluation.

Stage five

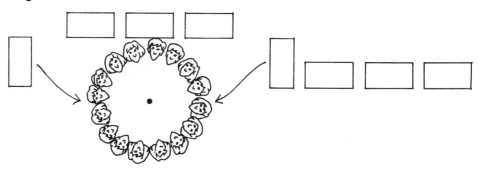

Working the pyramid stimulates *lots* of discussion. Even shy learners defend their decisions volubly against more extrovert learners.

Although as far as numbers are concerned this may at first seem a rather inflexible format for discussion, the teacher should have no problem with making simple adjustments; here we show what can be done if there is one learner too many, for instance.

Stage one

Stage two

Stage three

If there are exactly sixteen or thirty-two in the class, the teacher may still decide that it would take too long to complete the whole activity and will stop after stage 3 or stage 4.

The teacher will realise, of course, that it is much more important to engage the learners in a discussion than to get them into groups of a predetermined size. That is why she should not be deterred from situations in which there is one group too few at some stage.

In addition to a number of role-plays, simulations and discussions, *Getting Students to Talk* includes various follow-up activities. It should be remembered that all of them are entirely optional. Their aim is to help the teacher exploit the themes more fully — often by getting the learners to prepare a written exercise.

Quotations

Nowadays, proponents of communicative methods often say or imply that it is not very respectable to get your class to do oral drills, which are condemned as 'meaningless', 'boring', or 'uncommunicative'. Teachers have responded by (for example) setting oral exercises in which there is an 'information gap' ... Too often, though, these conscientious teachers set up communicative activities without first helping their pupils to overcome difficulties in pronunciation or giving them any controlled oral practice, because drills are out of favour. To hope that our pupils will learn English simply by being encouraged to communicate is, I suggest, to mistake *ends* for *means*. What is fallacious nowadays is the assumption that the new communicative techniques *displace* the older maniplative ones. Both sorts are needed. Pupils need first the chance to conquer formal difficulties and then the opportunity to exploit semantic possibilities. (Abbot 1981: 229).

If, after a simulation, the teacher says 'That simulation did not work well because the participants failed to find the most suitable answer', then this is a mistake of category; the teacher is confusing the simulation technique with other methods. In simulations generally, questions are more important than answers, and learning is more important than 'success'. (Jones 1982: 9).

In practice ... games and simulations ... have a role to play, but it cannot happily be a major role in a long-term language programme. Such techniques are frequently used with great success in short courses for intermediate and advanced adults and adolescents — but these are building on the basic work, however inadequate it may appear to be, of earlier teachers in more conventional schools. (Brumfit 1984: 82).

... The most common causes of potential chaos ...
The students don't understand the purpose and relevance of the activity.
Students waste time getting into groups and argue about who to work with. ...
Students fail to understand what to do.
Students can't remember what to do or who should be doing what. (Willis 1983: 32).

THE ROLE OF THE TEACHER

One of the reasons that learners are so often unsuccessful in real-life communication is that the types of interaction they are most used to are as follows:

1. Here is a teacher lecturing at a class (here of twelve learners). The interaction is all to the teacher or through the teacher.

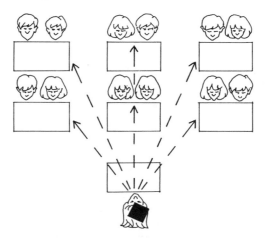

2. Here the teacher asks one of the learners to come to the front of the class and either listens to him or talks with him.

3. Here the teacher listens to or talks with one of the learners, who remains at his desk.

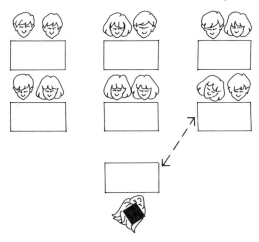

4. Here the teacher moves among the learners interacting with them individually.

5. Here the teacher asks two learners to speak to each other (e.g. present a dialogue they have learnt by heart).

If learners are asked to speak to each other they usually take turns in speaking rather than communicate. Moreover, the teacher is at hand, listening to everything that is being said.

These illustrations of some types of classroom interaction should help to show that in most cases only one interaction at a time takes place in the classroom and that the teacher is usually one of the interlocutors. The five diagrams depict types of interaction that are not necessarily unacceptable in themselves; the problem lies in maintaining an acceptable proportion of student talking time to teacher talking time and in providing a reasonable variety of techniques.

Here is a discussion in a traditional class.

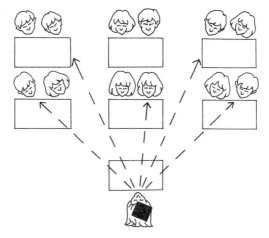

Although at a more advanced level the teacher is likely to organise discussions, too often the learners still talk to the teacher rather than to one another.

In the following illustrations we see the type of interaction that is appropriate for the activities in *Getting Students to Talk*.

With desks fixed

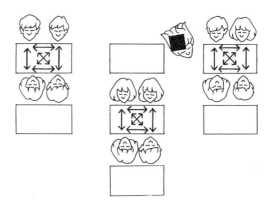

With desks moved: learners sitting in small circles

A communicative activity in a learner-centred class (see also *The Physical Layout of the Classroom*).

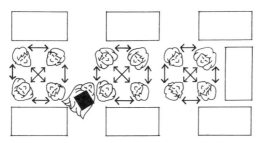

As can be seen, the teacher is free to listen, monitor, think ahead, re-plan the next stages and hear her learners teaching one another the vocabulary and grammar they know.

While communicative activities are in progress, the teacher no longer 'teaches': she organises, sets up activities and monitors them discreetly, i.e. listens to the learners and makes sure that everything is in order. The teacher should intervene only if she is quite certain that her learners cannot manage on their own.

The teacher should be like the conductor of an orchestra: conduct but not play. According to Jones (1981), the 'chief virtue [of simulations] is the removal of the teacher'.

Things to beware of

...The most common causes of potential chaos ...
    The teacher's instructions are too long and/or too complex to remember.
    The teacher keeps interrupting with more instructions or advice during the task.
    The teacher keeps correcting and demands too high a standard of accuracy.
    The teacher looks uninterested while group work is in progress and never smiles or encourages.
    (Willis 1983: 32).

ERRORS

Many teachers nowadays wrestle with the question whether it is fluency or accuracy in their learners' speech that is of paramount importance and thus whether they should or should not correct every error the learners make.

Many teachers opt for accuracy because

- accuracy is easier to define ('If the learner doesn't make any mistakes, his speech is accurate');
- it is easier to set up exercises and activities aimed at promoting accuracy (e.g. 'Change these sentences into reported speech and then tell me about Peggy's holiday plans');
- it is easier to grade for accuracy (e.g. 'You've made five mistakes, so you get +').

Adopting this teaching style entails the immediate correction of practically all the mistakes a learner makes. This in turn means that a lot of learners will be reluctant to speak for fear of making mistakes and being corrected.

Without going into the details of the relative advantage of both accuracy and fluency work, it seems reasonable to suggest that as there is a time and a place for everything, there should be a time for accuracy and a time for fluency. While the oral activities in *Getting Students to Talk* are meant for *fluency* work only, it is not suggested that correcting errors should be abandoned; rather it should be postponed until after the individual activities. Since learners generally expect to be corrected immediately and, if they are not, tend to think that the teacher has failed to notice their mistakes, it is most important to explain the rationale behind your actions — very explicitly if need be. For instance, you might say, 'In the next twenty minutes I want you to concentrate on speaking fluently. I will not stop you if you say something that is bad English. I will not correct any errors. I want you to speak, and to speak as quickly as you like.'

Before some ways of dealing with errors — after the end of an activity — are presented, it should be pointed out that sometimes teachers cannot correct mistakes for the simple reason that they are not aware of them. Although this might happen in grammatical exercises too, it is more likely to occur when both the learners and the teacher are geared towards fluency and communicativeness. If the teacher's native language is not English, it is quite easy to let errors arising from her mother tongue interference slip by unnoticed.

In order to deal with errors after an activity, the teacher first has to *remember* them. This can be done by tape-recording the discussion, then selectively transcribing from the tapes.

If tape recorders, tapes or time are limited, the teacher can use simple pencil-and-paper techniques. The easiest of these consists in jotting down the mistakes made by the learners, with or without their names. When the learners first notice that the teacher is standing next to them, listening and taking notes, they often feel inhibited. They soon grow used to it, however, and the teacher can take notes freely.

If it becomes apparent that many of the learners are making the same mistake, the teacher will probably want to devote one of the following lessons to remedial teaching. When, however, individual learners make individual mistakes, it can be useful to find out if those mistakes reflect the learners' imperfect knowledge of English ('errors of competence', according to S. Pit Corder's distinction) or carelessness at the production level ('errors of performance'). In other words, we all make mistakes even in our mother tongue when we are struggling to put our thoughts into words, e.g. sometimes we leave one sentence unfinished while we go on to say something else. Sometimes we are trying to express two thoughts at once and they come out jumbled. These are errors of performance. The speaker knows what is wrong and can correct it when it is drawn to his attention.

Errors of competence, on the other hand, are errors the speaker makes and doesn't know *are* errors because his knowledge and experience of the language are limited.

Here is a worked example of an error made during a role-play (*'I'll tell you when you'll phone me') and the process during the feedback session. The teacher reminds the learner of the sentence, e.g. Teacher, 'What did you 'What did you say about my phoning?'

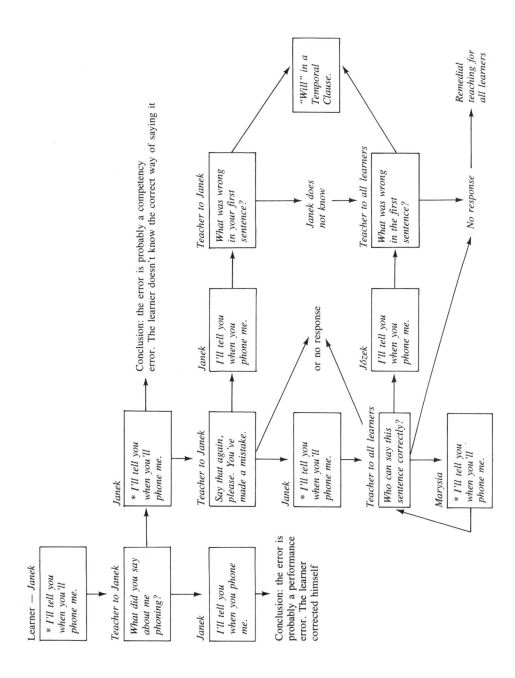

Once the learners get used to the idea of role-plays and simulations and this new procedure of correcting mistakes *after* the fluency period, they soon notice they are not being interrupted in the middle of a sentence because of a mistake. That awareness often helps them to become fully involved in what they are saying, and this in turn generates an increased number of mistakes. You do not need to be a teacher with audio-lingual leanings to wonder if it is acceptable for learners to speak worse English than usual. Stevick (Rivers and Temperley 1978: 60) reassures us very convincingly. According to him, mistakes are inevitable because of what he calls the 'SI line', SI standing for Simultaneous Interpretation. Simultaneous interpreters are efficient as long as they remain detached from what they are talking about. *Getting involved means making mistakes.* If we want our learners to be interested in what they are saying and to achieve genuine communication, we have to accept that their performance will be less perfect than in, say, a traditional grammar exercise. Stevick (Alatis 1976: 266) also warns us of 'lathophobic aphasia', i.e. 'unwillingness to speak for fear of making a mistake'. We are all familiar with this ourselves — we make more errors in our own language when we are very excited, and we get tongue-tied if lots of people are listening to us very critically.

Further perspectives on fluency and accuracy

We cannot afford to do nothing but accuracy-based work, for if we did we should never allow learners to act as genuine users at all. . . . No one can communicate naturally and at the same time concentrate on the form rather than on the content of their speech. (Finocchiaro and Brumfit 1983: 95).

For fluency work to be successful, the teacher should explain to the students why it is being encouraged and why they will benefit from not being corrected all the time. At the same time, teachers should provide specific sessions when correction of widely occurring errors (perhaps by very traditional procedures) will be made . . . Without . . . opportunities for correction, fluency practice runs the risk of producing nothing but a fluent classroom pidgin. (Finocchiaro and Brumfit 1983: 98).

There is no question of fluency being in any way a substitute for accuracy. Both are essential. . . . Right from the beginning of the course about a third of the total time could be spent on this sort of fluency activity, and the proportion will inevitably increase as time goes on. (Brumfit 1981: 7).

Students normally want some correction, and teachers should not refuse to correct all the time. (Brumfit 1981: 6).

One of the teacher's biggest difficulties is that the learner's speed of learning is different from the teacher's speed of teaching. What is needed can be described as 'a syllabus with gaps' or 'a syllabus with holes in it'. There will clearly have to be an important place in the syllabus for the introduction of new language, but there must also be extensive 'gaps' in which no new material is presented, but students are enabled to use effectively what they have learnt. (Brumfit 1981: 7).

HOME-MADE ACTIVITIES (MADE BY THE TEACHER)

Getting Students to Talk is a source of ideas that sooner or later will trigger off the teacher's own inventiveness. Here is an example of how the absurdities of everyday life can be easily translated into a role-play.

The idea of a scene entitled 'At the restaurant' is familiar to all. In L.G. Alexander's *Question and Answer* (Longman, 1967), one of the texts meant for listening comprehension is called 'What's for dinner?' and is an amusing story in which the waiter does not bother to update a menu. It is a rather traditional text, with nothing communicative about it. (Not that everything has always got to be communicative!)

Carol Livingstone's *Role Play in Language Learning* (Longman, 1983) includes a role-play that resembles Alexander's 'What's for dinner?' The waiter's role-card instructs him that 'The roast lamb is excellent. There is no salmon left'. One of the diners' role-card tells him he loves fish, while the other diner is a vegetarian. A menu has to be provided by the teacher with roast lamb and salmon marked on it. Considering the obvious built-in disagreement (see *Role-Plays, Simulations and Discussions* earlier in this section), we should have a ready conflict on our hands. However, the 1983 role-play is rather anaemic and the potential problem is not exploited to the full. The vegetarian might easily order an omelette or a salad and the fish-lover can find another fish dish. If we treat this role-play as a basis for a fairly ordinary dialogue, though, and not a fierce argument, everything is all right.

Now let us look at a home-made version of the same theme. The idea is practically the same: some dishes that appear on the menu are not available. The group of diners, which can be of any reasonable size, are given menus. The waiter has the same menu with some items crossed out and some extra ones added. The conversation proceeds along the usual lines. Role-cards are not necessary and the diners themselves decide what their likes are and how fussy they wish to be. It is quite easy to increase the learners' involvement even further by giving the waiter an opportunity briefly to double as the chef. First he decides which items on the menu are available and which are not, and then he is off to serve the diners! Haven't we all met situations in which a restaurant's menu is practically useless?

What about the actual food? We could have a menu with black caviar, lobster, etc. We could, however, have traditional local cuisine. When deciding which menu to choose, it is useful to remember that if at least one of the diners is a foreigner, an explanation of what certain local dishes are will be required. This becomes more 'real-life' the more the learners' own experiences are used.

HOME-MADE ACTIVITIES (MADE BY THE LEARNERS)

Home-made materials are best. 'Home-made' so far has meant 'designed by the teacher'. We can, however, go one step further and encourage the *learners* to prepare their own materials. This is one way of making learners more responsible for their own learning and for what is going on in the classroom. This is also one of the few cases when the learner is not working for the teacher, but for other learners. Moreover, what he is involved in will result in something *to be used*, rather than simply to remain 'work for work's sake'.

By preparing interesting materials, the learner is providing a challenge for his friends. To create such a challenge is a challenge in itself. This double challenge means stretching the learners' possibilities more effectively than the teacher could hope to do in practically any other situation.

Before the learners set out to prepare their own role-plays, the teacher should make sure that they know enough about the principles governing communicative activities. Here is what the teacher can do:

1. Choose a few role-plays (from this book and/or other sources) that the learners have done and that were particularly successful with them.
2. Ask the learners to analyse the individual role-plays as they remember them.

   ● What was the role-play about?
   ● Who were the participants?
   ● How were they characterised (if at all)?
   ● What kind of information were they provided with? Did all the participants know the same things?
   ● In what way did the role-play encourage the participants to talk?

3. Explain or elicit the concept of information gap and opinion gap (see *Role-Plays, Simulations and Discussions*).
4. Provide the learners with the full text of one of the role-plays they liked and let them analyse how the information/opinion gap is exploited.
5. Divide the learners into groups and ask each group to prepare one role-play. If learners lack ideas, the teacher can provide them with a selection of newspaper cuttings that might inspire them. Any unusual piece of information should help.
6. The groups present their role-plays to the others, who take part in them with no prior preparation. The other learners watch and listen.
7. The learners discuss the individual role-plays.

   ● Was the role-play successful?
   ● Why/why not?
   ● How was it constructed?
   ● Could it be improved?
   ● How?

LANGUAGE

Having a choice as to what one will say and how one will say it is one of the principles of real-life communication (Morrow 1981). That is why more expressions than are indispensable have been provided after most of the activities as well as in Part Three. That is also true of the vocabulary that appears after *Smoking*, for instance.

The language presented, however, is by no means exhaustive, so the teacher should feel free to expand the lists and comment on them. What the learners will probably need to be made aware of is that:

- the most widely applicable expressions have been chosen. Both very formal and very colloquial language has been avoided;
- the words and phrases grouped in frames are not necessarily synonyms. Furthermore, they might require different grammatical forms to follow them, e.g.

What would you say

about	
to	. . .

Learners should also be reminded that intonation can greatly change the meaning of practically any expression.

Everybody who has at one time or another attempted communicating in a foreign language knows that being lost for words is a fairly common experience. A good language learner, though, will try to manage without the exact word. This can be done in various ways depending on the kind of vocabulary item that has to be substituted.

It is important to stress at this point that not knowing (or not being able to recall) a lexical item is not necessarily an indication of a poor command of the language. Words that are relatively infrequent in everyday speech will often cause problems. Foreign learners should also be made aware that very often there are no one-to-one equivalents in two languages.

Asking about the meaning of a word, and defining

Sections of Part Three should help learners communicate without the exact word that is required, by following the stratagems used by native speakers. However, too colloquial words like *thingummajig, whatsisname* or *doo-da* should be discouraged, since when used by foreigners more often than not they sound out of place.

KEY TO SYMBOLS USED IN LAYING OUT THE USEFUL LANGUAGE ITEMS

Ø   indicates that the item/items in the frame can be omitted,
e.g. I'm │ so │ sorry
        │ Ø │

This means that both *I'm so sorry* and *I'm sorry* are permissible.

*   indicates that an incorrect form follows, e.g.
* *commit a suicide*.

/   stands for *or*, e.g. *he/she* stands for *he or she*.

Part Two
Role-Plays, Simulations and Discussions

To use this section read through each activity carefully. See what you need to prepare (e.g. how many copies of each role-card for the number of learners in your class). Think of the timing. The role-plays take 15–30 minutes on average. What will you do to prepare your learners? What will you do as a follow-up? Look through the *language* sections and look up the cross-references. Which expressions do your learners know well, which don't they know, and which are they unsure of? How will you prepare your students to use new expressions?

All these things a teacher must decide for herself. Only you know your learners and your situation. This book shares activities that can go well and are inherently communicative, but you know your own learners best.

A. ROLE-PLAYS

Each role-play is laid out as Procedure or Situation, Notes and Language. Where role-cards are needed, they are printed in full. Remember to remind the learner of the three rules: 'Don't show your card. Don't give all the information at once. Speak English.'

*****

1. PRESS CONFERENCE (for any number of learners)

Procedure
Learners choose a famous foreigner they would like to interview. One learner, preferably a volunteer, will role-play that person. A press conference is then set up with journalists (the rest of the learners) asking questions and the celebrity answering them. It does not matter if the answers have little in common with reality.

Notes
1. This is a role-play that does not require any role-cards.
2. In order to be really successful, this role-play should be as topical as possible, with currently popular singers, actors or athletes being interviewed.
3. The teacher can ask the learner who is to be interviewed to find as much as possible about the celebrity in advance, e.g. the day before the role-play.

Language useful for this role-play
Stalling for time

Well, | let me see   . . .
let's see
let me think
now
how shall I put it
how can I phrase this
Ø

Refusing to answer a question

If you don't mind	I'd rather not	say that
I think		answer that question
I'm afraid		tell you that
		discuss that subject

      .

I'd prefer not to | say that   .
answer that question
tell you that
discuss that subject

See also
LEADING TO A QUESTION (pages 33–34 and 156)
ASKING ABOUT PLANS (pages 126–127)
ASKING FOR OPINIONS (pages 142–143)
EXPRESSING OPINIONS (pages 142–143)
ASKING QUESTIONS ABOUT INTERESTS AND LIKES (pages 62 and 123–125)
ANSWERING QUESTIONS ABOUT INTERESTS AND LIKES (pages 62–63 and 123–125)
ASKING FOR CLARIFICATION (pages 141–142)
GIVING CLARIFICATION (pages 141–142)

2. WHY? (for groups of 2−4 learners)

> You and your colleagues are collaborating on a comprehensive book about the role of newspapers in everyday life. You are responsible for the section on classified advertisements.
>
> This is your first visit to this country and you have just received (as requested) some classified advertisements that have recently appeared in the press. You decide to interview the people who have placed them. In this way you hope to find out something about the role classified advertisements play in the everyday life of people who live here.

Procedure
1. The class is divided into journalists and people who have placed small advertisements. There should be one journalist for approximately every two people with the advertisements.
2. The journalists look at the advertisements and prepare the questions they will ask. In the meantime the other learners, who were either allotted or chose one advertisement each, think of the reasons why they placed them.
3. Each journalist meets two people and interviews them.
4. (optional) The journalists report (either orally or in writing) their findings, as if asked by the editor of the book they are working on.

Note
Rather than use the advertisements in this book, the teacher may ask her learners to bring into class some intriguing small advertisements they find for themselves and to use those.

Language
These are some of the questions that the journalists can ask:

Why did you place this advertisement?
Why are you looking for ...?
Is ... important for you? Why?
What will you do if you are not successful?

Each of these questions can be preceded by the following phrases. This will make the questions more polite.

Leading to a question
I hope you don't mind my asking, but ...

I wonder if | you'd allow me to / I could | ask a few | simple / Ø | questions ...

I wonder if you
| can |
| could |
| would be so kind as to |
spare me a minute or two

and answer a few questions.
I'd be interested to know why ...
I'm interested why ...
I'd like to know why ...

See also
INTRODUCING ONESELF (page 122)
LEADING TO A QUESTION (pages 128—130)
ASKING FOR CLARIFICATION (pages 141—142)
GIVING CLARIFICATION (pages 141—142)
STALLING FOR TIME (pages 32 and 154)
REFUSING TO ANSWER A QUESTION (pages 32 and 155)

*****

CLASSIFIED ADVERTISEMENTS

The following classified advertisements are used for several activities:

ACCOMMODATION OFFERED

• **Woman** 41 yrs, homely, vegetarian, non to occasional smoker, holistic care worker + cat require person of similar lifestyle to share spacious Clifton flat. £151 p.c.m. + bills. Helen Box 723.

• **One bedroom flat** in Clifton village to let. Newly decorated. £275 p.c.m. Box 893.

• **Third person** wanted to share friendly comfortable house in Easton. £120 p.c.m. excl. bills. Box 862.

• **Fishponds** Comfortable room in shared house. Gay man preferred. £30 p.w. incl. Box 72.

• **Eastville** Third person wanted to share house. £30 p.w. + bills. Must like dogs. Box 553.

• **Victoria Park** 3rd person wanted to share large comfortable C.H. house. £120 p.c.m. excl. of bills. Box 493.

• **Pleasant room**, shared house, Bedminster. Open fire to-boot. £100 p.c.m. plus bills. Jess Box 443.

• **Lodgings** offered to young discreet gay male, non-smoker. To share house with similar. £35 p.w. West Wilts. Box 457.

• **Fourth person** wanted to share comfortable house in Eastville. £90 p.c.m. Box 607.

• **I need** lively, positive person (plus child?) to share mortgage on Easton house (lots of potential) with me and my baby-to-come. Claire Box 138.

• **Room to let.** Share amenities in large house off Wells Road. Reasonable rent. Box 679.

• **Two rooms** in women's house, £28 p.w. Box 718.

• **Large sunny room** to let, shared modern house, Ashley Down. Non-smoker, vegetarian. £150 p.c.m. incl. Box 732.

• **Room** to let in friendly leftish house in Easton for professional with sense of humour. Preferably cat lover! £120 p.c.m. inclusive. Box 272.

• **West Bristol** Second person, non-smoker, twenties, to share comfortable house. Interest in music and Green issues desirable. Own large attractive room. £27 p.w. plus bills. Box 671.

• **Sociable socialist** to share house in Easton. Sunny room, nice garden, central heating, washing machine etc. £23 p.w. Box 420.

• **Female** wanted for room in shared flat. £78.45 p.c.m. Christian professional preferred. Box 743.

• **Redfield** Single room, nice house, female, veggie, non-smoker pref. £25 p.w. plus phone. Box 426.

● **Female** wanted to share quiet, friendly house in Horfield. £115 p.m. Non-smoker please. Box 057.

● **Short term let.** 2 bedroom cottage, city centre. Parking space. 2 weeks — 3 months. Contact Box 557.

● **Windmill Hill** Room in shared house. V. cosy. All mod cons. C.H., garden. For professional person. £120 p.c.m. plus one month's deposit. Box 666.

● **Montpelier** Employed non-smoking male. £30 inclusive. Box 476.

● **Two rooms** in smokeless spacious centrally heated house in Redfield (all mod cons) sharing with easy going vegetarianish ex-postgrad. £115, £100 p.c.m. + bills. Box 255.

● **Two rooms** available in lovely house in St Agnes — £110 p.c.m. each. Box 372.

● **Third person** wanted for mixed gay/straight household, St George. Pleasant room, warm comfortable house. £120 p.c.m. Box 561.

● **Windmill Hill** room in comfortable house. £25 p.w. Box 922.

ACCOMMODATION WANTED

● **Couple and cat,** sick of the city, looking for rural accommodation. Bristol/Bath area. Anything considered. Carole Box 194.

● **Council flat** exchange. Offer studio London, seek anything Bristol. Box 2614.

● **Homoeopath** (female) moving from Devon seeks rented accommodation. Box 427.

● **Sunny garden flat** for one or two. Box 138.

● **Visitors** require flat to rent May 10–24 Clifton/Cotham. Box 850.

SITUATIONS VACANT

WESTON COMMUNITY ASSOCIATION
requies a
**COMMUNITY DEVELOPMENT
WORKER**
(Part time — $18\frac{1}{2}$ hours)

To encourage community involvement so that all residents of Weston can benefit from living in a multi-racial area.

Salary: £8433–£9540 p.a. (Unqualified)
         £9909–£14,124 p.a. (Qualified)
         (pro rata and according to experience)

Details from: The Employment Secretary,
               Weston Community Association,
               15 Wood Lane,
               Weston

Weston Community Association is aiming to become an Equal Opportunities Employer and especially welcomes applications from people of Afro-Caribbean origin as they are under-represented in the workforce. (Section 38(1)(b) Race Relations Act applies)
Closing date: 17th May

Third woman
wanted to work part-time in
Green Bookshop Co-Op starting
July. 20–30 hrs per week, £3.75
per hr, under review. Send sae
for application form
from: Green Bookshop,
13 Well St,
Norwich

● **Central Community Advice Centre** . . . requires two Advice workers with experience, especially of welfare rights. Currently a 9 hour post very likely to increase to 15 hours. Salary (for 9 hrs) £2097.60 per annum. One vacancy is for temporary maternity cover until January. Closing date May 5th. Contact: CCAC, Community Association Building, Central Way, Sheffield.

**ESSEX COMMUNITY
THEATRE AGENCY**
requires
2 DRAMA WORKERS
(one female)
1 TECHNICIAN/DESIGNER
(to run workshops and facilitate productions with 14–21 year olds in Essex)
and
AN ADMINISTRATOR
All posts @ £8224.65 p.a.
Deadline 29th April
Details and application forms
from: ECTA, 3 End Lane
Chelmsford

ARCHITECTS PA

MD of a busy architectural practice seeks intelligent and numerate PA with good organisational ability
Salary negotiable around £10,000
Please write with C.V. to:
Geoffrey Todd
TODD LAMBERT
ARCHITECTS
Royal Colonnade
6 Park Street
Bristol

MISCELLANEOUS

DISCOVER a new social life, love or marriage. The most successful agency yet. Write to 'The ABC of LOVE', PO Box 909, Wellington, NZ

PERK UP your party with McKean's Music — classical to jazz. Box 806.

GRAPPELLI-STYLE QUARTERT/Trio available for all private functions. Sophisticated but fun. Box 230.

CROWD PULLERS: Events animated by brilliant street performers. Tel. 074.

KISSAGRAM LTD. Surprise someone today! Tel. 437.

CUTTING out meat? Read the bible 'Why You Don't Need Meat'. 'Crucial reading' — *City Limits*. 'Riveting' — *Elle*. Only £2.95 from Box 161.

WITCHCRAFT: what it is, how to make it work for you. Books/cassettes. Box 324.

FEMALE painter urgently needs £2,500 to start portrait painting business. Genuinely desperate. Please help if you can. Box 6912.

GENUINELY need £4,700 to clear debts and support wife and two young children. Will acknowledge. Box 6812.

DRAW CARTOONS. Learn by post from professionals. SAE for details. Box 281.

NO TEDDY BEAR'S PICNIC!
Play SKIRMISH
in woodlands near Beaconsfield.
Air-powered pistols, safety equipment
and lunch included.
Company games a speciality.
Weekdays or weekends.
Details Box 385.

UNATTACHED lady 52 seeks cultured humorous male for lasting relationship. London. Box 123.

TWO YOUNG entrepreneurs are looking for investors for equity investment scheme. Target profits of 400% annum. Low capital injections. More information, Box 861.

INNOVATIVE, inventive, mechanically minded, practical, widely experienced BSc in polymers seeks post. Box 7712.

DESKTOP Publishing Service. Icon graphics, typeset, design, layout and print anything from a letterhead or a CV to a novel. Magazines, newsletters, business presentations. Personalised stationery. One copy or a million. Box 691.

BRUTALLY ACCURATE Character Study. Have your prejudices confirmed. For free questionnaire ring 3763.

THE IMAGINARY JOURNEY — find a world you never knew existed. 325 (25p a minute cheap rate, 38p peak).

SKIN WITHOUT SPOTS — if you have tried everything and still have spots, blemishes, blackheads, acne, write to us for free advice and we will show you how easy it can be to have a clear and good-looking skin. You'll be glad to have found us. Send SAE: SKIN CONSULTANTS. Box 272.

IF ALCOHOL DAMAGES your work or your family life, for confidential advice and treatment involving NO absence from work, contact the Medical Director, Health Unit, Box 713.

HANDWRITING ANALYSIS. Send SAE for free brochure. Box 811.

HOUSE OF COLOUR West End. Colour and style analysis. Let us show you how to always look your best by choosing the right colours and style for your individual skin tone and body shape. Ring LIZ on 4558.

WANT A character report on anyone? Send handwriting sample, whether writer male or female, left or right handed, first name and £5 to PETER COLLINS, Box 901.

COMPUTER Astrology. Personal horoscope, forecast and birth chart. Send date, time and place of birth with £12.50 to: GEOFF LORD, Box 442.

PLANT A BLUEBELL WOOD. 1000 seeds £7. 250 seedlings £9.50, £24 per 1000. 100 snowdrop bulbs £7, 500 for £26. Box 329.

PENFRIENDS — USA. Make lasting friendships through correspondence. Send age, interests. Free reply. Box 822.

THE FOREMOST JOURNAL of strange phenomena — sample copy only £1.75 from: Box 961.

BALLSLIP JUGGLERS! Learn to juggle expertly in just four weeks. Guaranteed correspondence course reveals secrets. Free details write now: Box 322.

INDIA: Don't just watch, get involved! Experience real local life in the homes and palaces, tropical backwaters and deserts. 7-week expeditions. Box 947.

BRITTANY — 300-year-old farmhouse. Sleeps up to 10. Details: FRENCH TRAVEL, Box 256.

HOW AND where to raise the capital you need to start a business. This authoritative book shows you how. £10 inc postage. Details from Box 311.

AFRICA — Safari Camping Adventure Holidays, 1–4 weeks from £415, 7–19 weeks from £1,840. We offer the most comprehensive holidays available. Full details in our full-colour brochure: AFRICAN EXPEDITIONS LTD. Box 271.

3. LINGUA FRANCA (for pairs of learners)

A new and rather controversial school of foreign languages has recently come into operation. It guards its secret very carefully, so, apart from its advertising campaign and some 'Situations Vacant' advertisements, very little is known about its operation. All the learners read all six advertisements before they are given their role-cards.

Advertisements

English Bulgarian Chinese Danish Japanese German French and others	Fast-speed tapes Rhythmic breathing The rapid way to learn languages LANGUAGE→FAST Guaranteed success	LINGUA FRANCA 99 Jubilee Street, W.11 Tel 462-3958

Greek Spanish Icelandic Italian and others	The super new method called 'Three and a half days' from the USA LANGUAGE→FAST Individual attention at all times	LINGUA FRANCA 99 Jubilee Street, W.11 Tel 462-3958

Latin Maltese Portuguese Norwegian Polish Russian and others	Total knowledge induced in easy stages Just close your eyes and learn! LANGUAGE→FAST Our students never fail	LINGUA FRANCA 99 Jubilee Street, W.11 Tel 462-3958

Swahili Swedish Tamil Urdu Serbo-Croat Greek and others	Telepathic conversation techniques Instant communication Your speed of learning will amaze you! Why not learn two languages at once LANGUAGE→FAST You can't find a better method	LINGUA FRANCA 99 Jubilee Street, W.11 Tel 462-3958

Teacher wanted, Private Language School LINGUA FRANCA. We will train you in our new methods. You must be receptive, flexible, attractive and fast-thinking phone 462-3958

Secretary/Receptionist. Are you lively persuasive, attractive? We pay generous salary for 25 hours a week, private language school LINGUA FRANCA, phone us and persuade us to interview you 462-3958

Role-cards

The students make pairs. Reporter A and Learner; Reporter B and Owner; Reporter C and Teacher. The Reporters do the interviewing.

Reporter A. You are a reporter who has been assigned the task of preparing a series of ten-minute broadcasts for a programme for the learners of English in your country. You have decided to devote a programme to LINGUA FRANCA, the new school of foreign languages. You want to start with an interview with a typical learner of English. You can ask other reporters to prepare additional interviews for the programme (e.g. with an average teacher of English or the owner of LINGUA FRANCA).

Learner. You are learning English. You have been chosen to take part in a radio broadcast on LINGUA FRANCA, the new school of foreign languages. You are a typical student (you are learning English at evening classes, at another school). Express your opinion of LINGUA FRANCA. (You have seen the advertisements only.)

Reporter B. You have been asked to collaborate on a series of ten-minute broadcasts for a programme for the learners of English in your country. Your task is to interview the owner of LINGUA FRANCA.

Owner. You are the owner of LINGUA FRANCA, the new school of foreign languages. You are going to be interviewed in connection with your school which you are rather proud of.

Reporter C. You have been asked to collaborate on a series of ten-minute broadcasts for a programme for the learners of English in your country. Your task is to find out what an average teacher of English thinks about the new school which is advertised in such an intriguing way. The interview will be used in the programme.

Teacher. You have been chosen to take part in a radio broadcast on LINGUA FRANCA, the new school of foreign languages. You are an average foreign language teacher (you teach English at a secondary school). Express your opinion of LINGUA FRANCA. (You have seen the advertisements only.)

Notes

1. The role of the owner of LINGUA FRANCA is the most difficult one, since it requires a great deal of inventiveness.
2. Some learners might insist that not much can be said about a school nobody knows anything about. In cases like this, the teacher can make a few general suggestions along the following lines.

   - The *owner* should think of a justification and explanation of the claims made in the advertisements, which is precisely what *reporter B* will most likely be interested in.
   - *Reporter A* can ask about the *learner's* experience with foreign languages, about the methods used in other schools, like the learner's school and whether he/she would like to take a course at LINGUA FRANCA instead.
   - *Reporter C* can ask the *teacher* what he/she thinks of the claims put foward by LINGUA FRANCA, what method he/she finds most effective and whether he/she would be tempted to answer the 'Situations Vacant' advertisement.

3. As an optional follow-up activity the *reporters* can compare their findings and prepare a panel discussion, in which all the participants take part. The discussion has to be rehearsed.
4. Instead of a panel discussion (or, alternatively, on the basis of it) a short article is prepared. The learners cooperate on it.

Language

Expressing supposition

I expect ...

I wouldn't be surprised if ...

I suppose ...

I don't suppose ...

What this probably means is ...

That might mean that ...

I don't know, but ...

See also

INTRODUCING ONESELF (page 122)

LEADING TO A QUESTION (pages 33−34, 128−130 and 156)

ASKING FOR OPINIONS (pages 142−144)

EXPRESSING OPINIONS (pages 142−144)

ASKING FOR CLARIFICATION (pages 141−142)

GIVING CLARIFICATION (pages 141−142)

STALLING FOR TIME (pages 32 and 154)

REFUSING TO ANSWER A QUESTION (pages 32 and 155)

*****

4. PERSIAN RUGS (for groups of 3−4 learners)

The Hull Trading Company Ltd intends to buy Persian rugs for the home market. Two offers have been short-listed, one much cheaper than the other. A decision as to which offer will be accepted has to be reached at today's meeting.

> **Charles/Christine Abbott.** In your opinion Persian rugs are the best possible business at the present moment. It is quite obvious to you that the cheaper rugs should be bought. Do not agree to anything else. You suspect that Bale has been promised a commission from one of the manufacturers.

> **Simon/Sue Bale.** In your opinion Persian rugs are the best possible business at the moment.

You think that the quality and the design are much more important than the price. In this case the quality and design coincide with a higher price. You are sure that the price will not deter your prospective customers. You realise you are suspected of agreeing on a commission from one of the manufacturers but in fact this is not true.

Mark/Martha Collins. You do not know much about trade. You got your job with HTC quite by chance and now you are afraid people will find out you are not properly qualified. You talk a lot and try to please everybody.

Alan/Ann Dell. You have doubts whether there is a home market for Persian rugs and so whether they should be bought at all. The company could make much more money on Dutch tulips. You dislike people who try to ingratiate themselves with everybody.

Note
The role of Dell is optional.

Language
Expressing disagreement in a discussion
Wouldn't it be rather risky to ...?
You haven't convinced me that ...
Isn't that out of the question?
I can't accept that.
Do you expect me to believe that?
No way.
What an absurd idea!

See also
MAKING EVERYBODY ACTIVE (pages 69 and 151)
THE LANGUAGE OF DISCUSSION (pages 141−152)

5. RETIREMENT (for groups of 3–6 learners)

At the end of the year, Edith Ray will retire after twenty years as secretary to the director of DOG Ltd, a small company dealing in electrical equipment. Traditionally a farewell party would have been organised, but recently this practice has been discontinued as the parties used to take place during office hours. Some say that Mrs Ray's approaching retirement is a good opportunity to establish a new way of expressing appreciation to those who have worked for DOG Ltd for several years. The employees of one of the departments have gathered in order to discuss the issue.

A

> Mrs Ray has always been very friendly and helpful. True, one sometimes gave her presents but don't we all accept presents from time to time?

B

> If somebody is retiring, they deserve a farewell present, no matter what they are like. Personally you are not too keen on Mrs Ray, but will *not* giving her a present change anything?

C

> A lot of derogatory things that are said about Mrs Ray are true. Still, as a senior employee of the company, you happen to remember the previous secretary, who was much worse.

D

> Mrs Ray is a widow, all on her own. Her private life is very lonely and sad. It seems particularly important to say goodbye to her in an exceptionally warm way, no matter what kind of an employee and colleague she has been.

a
> Once, when you needed help badly, Mrs Ray refused to help unless you gave her a bribe. Mrs Ray did not say that in so many words but her meaning was quite unambiguous.

b
> You have only recently come to work for DOG Ltd and have hardly had time to meet Mrs Ray properly. She seems an ill-natured type of person, however.

c
> Knowing what Mrs Ray was like, ten years ago you gave her a big box of chocolates. You asked her to help you in getting a promotion. She took the chocolates but you are still where you were before.

d
> You do not understand why people should be given farewell presents. They were paid for the jobs they were doing.

Notes

1. Roles marked with upper-case letters (A, B, C and D) are those in favour of giving Mrs Ray a present. Roles with lower-case letters (a, b, c and d) are those against the idea. Depending on the number of learners in particular groups, the teacher should select an appropriate number of role-cards. She should also make sure that the groups are not too big, i.e. 4–6 people, and that the positive and negative roles are fairly evenly matched.

2. Once the learners have performed the role-play and have thus practised presenting arguments in this type of situation, the teacher can repeat the role-play with a different set of role-cards (see next page) for groups of 3–4, preferably with different learners in the group compared to the A–D and a–d role-play. This time the roles are much more flexible and the learners have to think of their own arguments. If you need to increase the size of the groups at this stage, additional copies of role-card II can be prepared. If one role-card has to be left out (e.g. with any group of only three learners) omit role-card I.

I

> The whole discussion is a waste of time. In an office one should work and not talk oneself out of breath. The problem is non-existent. Either you give Mrs Ray a present or you do not. What difference does it make?

II

> Deciding whether to give Mrs Ray a present or not is a good opportunity to have a chat rather than to work. You do not care if she gets one or not. Try to prolong the discussion.

III

> You have nothing against Mrs Ray but, as it happens, you are rather short of money, so you do not like the idea of giving her a present. (You are a heavy gambler but do not tell anybody. Think of a reason for not giving a present.)

IV

> You have never really had anything to do with Mrs Ray and you do not care if she gets a present or not. However, you will be retiring next year and you would not mind getting a handsome farewell present. You know that giving Mrs Ray a present will set a precedent, so if she gets a present, you will too. (Do not say that to the others. Think of a different reason for giving a present.)

Language
Some useful phrases:

What do you	think	we should do	?
	suggest	should be done	

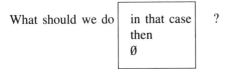

What are we going to do about | all this / this business | ?

See also
MAKING EVERYBODY ACTIVE (pages 69 and 151)
EXPRESSING DISAGREEMENT IN A DISCUSSION (pages 41 and 148)
THE LANGUAGE OF DISCUSSION (pages 141–152)

*****

6. SCRIBA (for groups of 2–3 learners)

All learners should first see the advertisement

> **SCRIBA** SITUATIONS WANTED?
> SITUATIONS VACANT?
> **SCRIBA** will help you write your advertisement.
> **SCRIBA** will help you write your letter of application.
> Your curriculum vitae will look much better with **SCRIBA**'s help.
> Our trained and friendly staff at **SCRIBA** will help you write any letters
> in English — love letters, letters of complaint, anything!
> **SCRIBA** tel: 493-9765.

Role-cards

A

> You work for SCRIBA. Your work involves
> assisting clients. You are eager to help them as
> your pay depends on the number of letters and
> applications you write. Moreover, SCRIBA is a
> new company, so it is particularly important to
> establish a good reputation.

B

> Choose an advertisement for a job you would like
> to have. Decide who you are and what you can
> do. Go to SCRIBA and ask them to write a job
> application for you.

C

> You have just come back from a rather badly-run foreign language course. (Decide why you did not like the course.) It is very important for you to remain on good terms with the foreign organisers of the course, so you have decided to write a letter expressing your appreciation. Ask SCRIBA to write the letter for you.

D

> You have a cousin you have never met and who lives in New Zealand. Your mother insists that you write to him at least once a year. You cannot be bothered to write a letter yourself. Ask SCRIBA to help you.

E

> You want to answer the following advertisement:
>
> > New company setting up in export—import. We are looking for enterprising people with languages to join our staff. Good pay and lots of opportunities. Box number 548969.
>
> Prepare your biography (age, education, languages, work experience, etc.) as well as other important details, such as what kind of enterprise you would be interested in, what role you would expect to play in the company and why you might be useful. Remember that your application should be as interesting as possible in order to attract the advertiser's attention. Ask SCRIBA to help you.

F

You want to answer the following advertisement:

> Wanted, a French-speaking nanny for a three-year-old boy. Send application and references to box number 430060.

You do not speak any French but your English is quite fluent. You have just completed a course for kindergarten teachers but you have no practical experience. The only references you can present are from the course organisers. You are very shy and insecure. Even though you speak English, you do not feel up to writing a convincing application in that language yourself. You have decided to come to SCRIBA and let them write it for you.

G

> **DISCOVER** a new social life, love or marriage. The most successful agency yet. Write to 'The ABC of LOVE', PO Box 909, Wellington, N.Z.

You would like to meet new people through this agency. You are very impatient and you get annoyed quite easily. You have come to SCRIBA to ask them to write a letter to 'The ABC of LOVE'. You think that the person who is supposed to write it for you at SCRIBA is most incompetent.

Think of all the relevant details of your life. They should be included in your letter.

H

You are a 45-year-old university graduate. You have been working for a foreign trade enterprise for fifteen years. You have never held any significant posts, even when you worked in Romania for two years. You have spent four months in New York working as a cook in an Italian restaurant. You speak English and some Russian. You also have a smattering of Romanian. You want to apply for a job with 'MART'. Ask SCRIBA to help you write an application. (Prepare the missing details of your biograph.)

> At MART International Enterprise we are expanding our local base. We are looking for new employees with experience of international trade. MART staff are hard-working, outgoing, young, fluent in several languages, keen to take responsibility, and always willing to see each deal through to a successful conclusion. Does that description fit you? If so, write with full details of your experience, languages, travel, trading skills, contacts and ambitions to: MART Personnel, 42 Solar Street, N.12.

I

You have a rather shy brother, whom you would like to see married as soon as possible. Unfortunately, he does not get along with women very well. He has never even had a girlfriend. You think that placing a lonely hearts advertisement in an Australian magazine might solve the problem. Your brother does not know you have come to SCRIBA and that you want to place an ad in his name.

Remember that if your brother is to find a wife, the ad has to be as appealing as possible. You are eager to get him married because your wife/husband detests him and this animosity is a strain on your otherwise happy marriage. Some details about your brother (think of any other relevant ones, e.g. name; Zodiac sign): height — 1.60 m; weight — 80 kg; hair — fair (growing bald); eyes — grey; age — 44; education — primary; occupation — postman; interests — horse-racing, drinking beer, watching television.

Notes

1. In every pair of learners taking part in this role-play, one should be given the role of a SCRIBA employee (role-card A) and the other the role of a client (role-cards B—I).
2. If two or more pairs of learners work with the same role-cards, e.g. A and F or A and I, Fs' application or Is' ads can be compared.
3. In order for the SCRIBA employees (role-card A) to deal with clients B, E, F and H, they have to know how to write letters of application. If they do not, it is enough for them to fill in a job application form (see below).
4. If there is an odd number of learners, either a client can come with a friend or two SCRIBA employees can assist one client.

A job application form

Family Name:
First Name/s:
Day, Month, Year and Place of Birth:
Nationality:
Marital Status:
Children:
Address and Telephone Number:
Education and Professional Training:
dates — schools, courses, etc. — qualifications:

Particulars of Career:
dates — places of work — positions

Foreign Languages:
state the degree of fluency

Other Relevant Details:

When is the Applicant Willing to Start Work:
When is the Applicant Available for Interview:
Type of Work Preferred:
Special Requirements:

Language

This is one of the patterns a conversation at the SCRIBA office might follow:

SCRIBA employee:

What can I do for you, | madam | ?
| sir |

SCRIBA client:

I wonder if you could help me: | I'd like to apply for a job.
| I'd like to send a letter.
| I'd like to place an advertisement.

SCRIBA employee:

We'll certainly do our best, | madam | .
| sir |

Can you give me the details, please?

Can you show me the advertisement | you'd like | to answer?
| you wish |

What would you like to say in | your | advertisement | ?
| the | letter |
| | application |

SCRIBA client: (provides the details and then asks)

What else do you think I should | include in my application | ?
| include in my advertisement |
| write in my letter |

SCRIBA employee:

Can you think of any other | relevant | details | ?
| important | pieces of information |

Is there anything else | we | can do for you, | madam | ?
| I | | sir |

See also
ASKING FOR ADVICE (page 78)
OFFERING ADVICE (page 78)
ASKING FOR HELP (pages 128−130)
EXPRESSING SUPPOSITION (pages 40 and 156)

*****

7. WORX (for groups of 2−3 learners)

A

> You work for WORX, a private employment agency. Your job requires helping to find both employers and employees for your clients (who in most cases contact you by telephone). You depend on the commission you get, so you have to make sure you keep everybody happy. When a client calls you, 1. complete Form A or Form B; 2. consult the appropriate classified advertisements, which constitute your file; 3. suggest at least one job or employee, as the case may be.

B

> Decide on a job you would like to have and the things you can do and are good at. Phone WORX, a private employment agency, and find out if they have a suitable job for you.

C

> You can speak English quite well but your spelling is poor. You are good with numbers and you can type a little. You are looking for a job with travelling prospects. You rather like the idea of working with foreigners. Phone WORX, a private employment agency, and find out if they have a suitable job for you.

D

> You are looking for an employee for your company. WORX, a private employment agency, has been recommended to you. Phone the agency and ask if they have somebody suitable. Insist on receiving exhaustive information. You have a habit of saying everything twice, rephrasing your words only slightly. Remember to decide first what job you are offering and what qualifications you expect.

Form A

SITUATION WANTED

Family Name:
First Name/s:
Age:
Telephone Number:
Education:

Qualifications:

Experience:

Typing:
Driving Licence:
Foreign Languages:
Other Relevant Details:

Requirements:
type of job — pay — hours — benefits

When is the Applicant Willing to Enter Employment:
When is the Applicant Available for Interview:

Form B

SITUATION VACANT

Employer:
name of person and/or company

Telephone Number:
Requirements:
age of applicant
education
qualifications
experience
skills (typing, driving, cooking, etc.)
foreign languages
other

Conditions:
type of job
pay
hours
benefits
other

When Does the Job Commence:
When Will the Interview Take Place:

Notes

1. In every pair of learners taking part in this role-play, one should be given the role of a WORX employee (role-card A) and the other the role of a client (role-cards B, C or D).
2. If there is an odd number of learners, either a client can come with a friend, or two WORX employees can assist one client.
3. The classified advertisements are on page 35.
4. To role-play talking on the telephone the two learners should sit next to each other, but back to back so they cannot see each other's face, but can hear each other's voice.

Language

Some questions the WORX employee might find useful

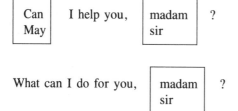

| Can | I help you, | madam | ? |
| May | | sir | |

| What can I do for you, | madam | ? |
| | sir | |

When talking to a prospective employee

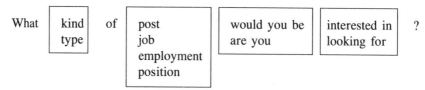

What	kind	of	post	would you be	interested in	?
	type		job	are you	looking for	
			employment			
			position			

What are your qualifications?

| Have you | got | any relevant | experience | ? |
| | Ø | | training | |

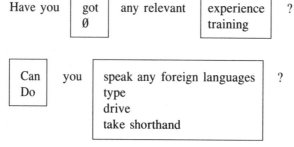

Can	you	speak any foreign languages	?
Do		type	
		drive	
		take shorthand	

What foreign languages do you speak?
Have you got a driving licence?

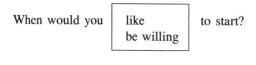

| When would you | like | to start? |
| | be willing | |

| When | could | you start? |
| | can | |

When | would | you be available for an interview?
     | will
     | could
     | can

When talking to a prospective employer
What are your requirements?

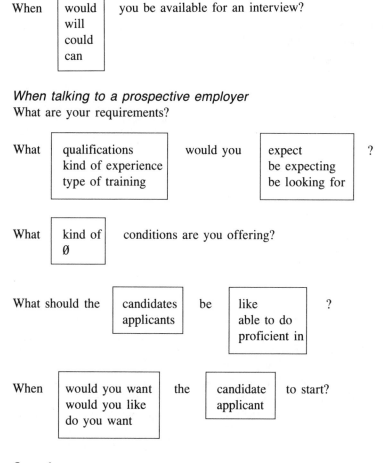

What | qualifications | would you | expect | ?
     | kind of experience | | be expecting
     | type of training | | be looking for

What | kind of | conditions are you offering?
     | Ø

What should the | candidates | be | like | ?
                | applicants | | able to do
                | | | proficient in

When | would you want | the | candidate | to start?
     | would you like | | applicant |
     | do you want |

See also
TALKING ON THE TELEPHONE (page 139)

8. BARBARA AND ANNA (for pairs of learners)

Barbara and Anna will soon complete their education. They have just started looking for jobs. Both of them speak good English and can type. Here are the 'Situations Vacant' advertisements they have found.

A
> Male English teacher requires young female secretary, part-time or full-time, evenings. Send photo with application. Box 55435.

C
> Summer work July/August visiting Canadian businessman making a detailed report on local market potential needs secretary willing to arrange travel and interviews and type reports. Box 532232.

B
> Doctor treating international patients needs temporary keyboard operator (word processor) to key in records of patients. Four months approximately. Hours negotiable. Write Box 532143.

D
> International bookshop requires good organiser to run stock and ordering. Fluent English, good on the telephone, meticulous record-keeping, flexible hours, excellent pay. Box 438769.

Points to consider

A. Why should a teacher need a secretary? How can he afford one? Even if he can afford a secretary, he will not be able to pay her much. Why does the secretary have to be young? Shouldn't qualifications be more important than age? There is something suspicious about this advertisement.

B. This job is not very ambitious but would you really be able to cope with a more challenging one? It is a temporary job, which can be both an advantage and a disadvantage. Some money would certainly come in handy but this job is not likely to be a well-paid one.

C. Is it a good idea to give up your last long holiday for a temporary job? Once you start working, your holidays will be much shorter.

D. What does being a good organiser really mean? Are you a good organiser? How will your prospective employers want to check that? There is bound to be stiff competition.

> **Barbara.** You and your friend have met to discuss your future jobs. You think that Anna would like you to help her decide which job she should apply for. Expecting you to do that is rather surprising, since you are looking for a job yourself and both of you might find yourselves competing for the same vacancy.
> 1. Make up your mind which job you will apply for. Choose one only. Do not tell Anna what your choice is.

2. Discuss the jobs with Anna. Some points to consider are suggested; think of other ones yourself, particularly those in favour of the jobs.
3. Find out which advertisement Anna will answer.

Anna. You and your friend have met to discuss your future jobs. You think that Barbara would like you to help her decide which job she should apply for. Expecting you to do that is rather surprising, since you are looking for a job yourself and both of you might find yourselves competing for the same vacancy.

1. Make up your mind which job you will apply for. Choose one only. Do not tell Barbara what your choice is.
2. Discuss the jobs with Barbara. Some points to consider are suggested; think of other ones yourself, particularly those in favour of the jobs.
3. Find out which advertisement Barbara will answer.
4. Begin the conversation by talking about the first advertisement.

Notes

1. On no account should the participants realise that their role-cards are virtually identical. The learners work in pairs: one is Barbara, the other is Anna.
2. It is up to the teacher whether to specify what kind of education the girls are about to complete or not. The girls can be finishing a secondary school, a post-secondary school or graduating from a university. The choice will not affect the role-play in any significant way.
3. One or both of the participants may be male, e.g. 'Alan' and 'Bob' while the advertisements remain unchanged. This means there will be at least one additional point to consider, namely what chances a male applicant could have.
4. Other 'Situations Vacant' advertisements can be used, with different points to consider suggested.
5. As a homework assignment the learners can be asked to write a letter of application for the job they have chosen. The letters can then be compared and discussed.

Language
Asking about plans and replying evasively
Have you got any plans?
Have you made any plans yet?

No, not really. | What | about you?
                | How |

Have you got anything in mind?

| Well | | special | | What | about you?
No	, nothing	in particular	.	How
Oh		worth talking about		
		worth mentioning		

What are you planning to do?

I don't know yet. | What | about you?
                  | How |

BE CAREFUL:
In English Anna is pronounced |ˈænə|.

See also
EXPRESSING INDECISION (page 151)
EXPRESSING SUPPOSITION (pages 40 and 156)
ASKING ABOUT PLANS (page 126)
RESPONDING to the above — NOTHING DEFINITE (page 127)

9. CAN YOU COOK? (for groups of three learners)

> Busy diplomat and wife need a live-in domestic help, smart, neat, fluent in English and capable of all normal household chores. No children, but a large house with frequent social functions. Write with references to McDonald, 17 Celebration Square, Central 3.

Mrs McDonald. You want to know as much as possible about Teresa's background and experience (age, education, likes and dislikes, hobbies, experience in cooking and housework, etc.). You are suspicious about the answers Teresa is giving you. Ask the same questions twice and compare the answers. You can see that your husband finds Teresa attractive. You are afraid he will have yet another affair.

Mr McDonald. You like Teresa very much. You think she is rather attractive. You want her to get the job. Try to persuade your wife to take her on (without making her suspicious about your motives). You are annoyed by practically everything your wife says.

Teresa. You are a university graduate. You are bored with your present job (decide what it is). You want to mix with diplomats, perhaps marry one and go abroad. You think that this job can help you. You live with your mother and you have never had to do any cooking or housework. You think that the McDonalds are slightly strange but you are prepared to tolerate them as you are desperate to change your job.

Language

Here are some of the things that Mr and Mrs McDonald might expect Teresa to do:

make the beds every day
change the bedclothes every week

cook
prepare

all the meals

wait at table three times a day
wash and dry the dishes after every meal

do the

washing
ironing

every week

go to the dry-cleaner's once in a while
polish the shoes regularly
mop the kitchen floor whenever necessary

vacuum
hoover

the carpets every other day

shampoo the carpets periodically

dust
polish

the furniture every so often

wash
clean
scrub

whatever needs

washing
cleaning
scrubbing

tidy the house
do the shopping

water
weed

the garden occasionally

mow the lawn from time to time

See also

ASKING QUESTIONS ABOUT LIKES AND DISLIKES (pages 62 and 123—125)
ANSWERING QUESTIONS ABOUT INTERESTS AND LIKES (pages 62—63 and 123—125)
ASKING ABOUT PLANS (pages 58 and 126—127)
SOME QUESTIONS AN EMPLOYEE CAN BE ASKED (pages 54 and 137—138)

10. MARRY ME (for groups of 3−4 learners)

Mr O'Hara and the women meet in a café.

Mr O'Hara. You are Australian. You want to marry a women from England. You are talking to the candidates now. You want to learn as much as possible about them. You realise they might be telling you all sorts of things (not necessarily the truth!) to marry you and start a new life as an Australian. You are soon leaving to return to Australia so you must make up your mind now. You begin.

Sophia. You think that all men fish for compliments, want women to agree with them in everything, etc. Pretend to be a stupid, naive woman whose only concern will be to look after her husband. You desperately want to get married to this Australian and go to Australia. Make him like you and not the others (make fun of them, etc.).

Christina. You think that all men like very intelligent, experienced and independent women from whom they can learn things. You desperately want to get married to this Australian and go to Australia. Make him like you and not the others (make fun of them, etc.).

Maria. You desperately want to get married to this Australian and go to Australia. You realise the other candidates are putting on an act. Your only chance to attract him is to make him understand that they are lying. Be natural and do not pretend anything.

Note
The role of Maria is optional.

Language
Asking yes/no questions about interests and likes

Are you | interested in / keen on | ... ?

Do you | like / enjoy | ... ?

Do you take much interest in ... ?

Have you | got / Ø | any favourite ... ?

Asking wh- questions about interests and likes

What | are / is | your favourite ... ?

What | kind / Ø | of ... do you | like best / like / enjoy most / enjoy | ?

What | kind of / Ø | ... are you | interested in / keen on | ?

Answering yes/no questions about interests and likes

Yes, | as a matter of fact / actually / Ø | | I do / I am |

Yes, very much | indeed / Ø | .

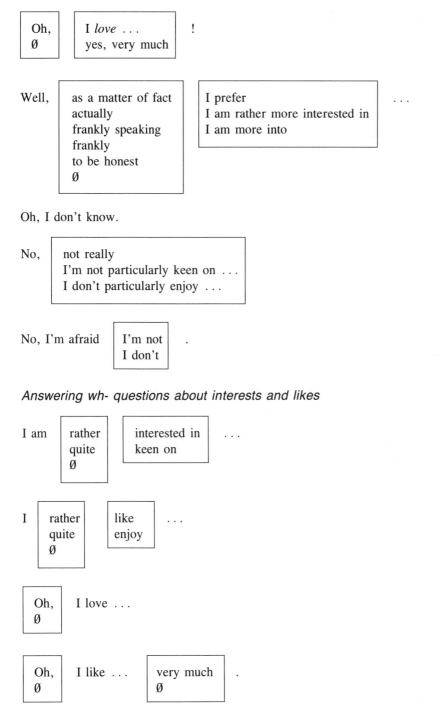

| Oh, Ø | I *love* . . . yes, very much | ! |

| Well, | as a matter of fact actually frankly speaking frankly to be honest Ø | I prefer I am rather more interested in I am more into | . . . |

Oh, I don't know.

| No, | not really I'm not particularly keen on . . . I don't particularly enjoy . . . |

| No, I'm afraid | I'm not I don't | . |

Answering wh- questions about interests and likes

| I am | rather quite Ø | interested in keen on | . . . |

| I | rather quite Ø | like enjoy | . . . |

| Oh, Ø | I love . . . |

| Oh, Ø | I like . . . | very much Ø | . |

Expressing agreement with somebody's likes

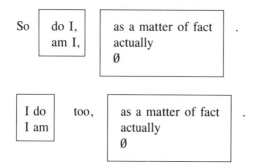

Expressing agreement with somebody's dislikes

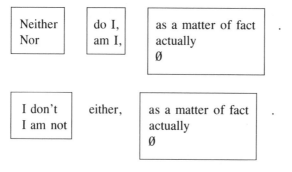

BE CAREFUL:

1. Except for a very limited number of situations, it is impolite to say 'of course' when answering somebody's questions.
2. The use of 'love' to express strong likes (e.g. 'I love tennis') is used especially by girls and women.

11. EXPECTATIONS (for groups of 3—4 learners)

> **Mr Bolton.** Your daughter Susan is expecting a baby. You are delighted. You think that it is never too early to start making important plans. You think that if it is a boy, a proper school (a good knowledge of Latin!) is the only basis for a future career as a lawyer, doctor or diplomat. If it is a girl, she should speak foreign languages, sing and play the piano very well. In this way she will find a good husband. You start the conversation.

> **Mrs Bolton.** Your daughter Susan is expecting a baby. You are delighted. You think that Martin and Susan are old enough to be left alone to decide on their baby's future. Anyway, it is bad luck to plan the future of an unborn baby. (Do not tell the others about your superstition because they are bound to laugh at you.) Last night you had a dream and you are sure this will be a boy. You think your husband talks too much. Try to change the subject of the conversation.

> **Mr Jenkins.** Your daughter-in-law Susan is expecting a baby. You are delighted. You do not believe in schools at all. They ruin natural talents. You think that if your grandchild is left alone, he or she will spontaneously become a great artist. It does not matter whether the baby is a boy or a girl.

> **Mrs Jenkins.** Your daughter-in-law Susan is expecting a baby. You are delighted. You think that Martin and Susan are far too young and inexperienced to decide about the future of your

granddaughter. (You are sure it will be a girl!) You think she should become a second Madame Curie. You have already bought her a 'Young Chemist' set.

Note

In the case of too few learners available to take part in the role-play, one of the role-cards can be left out (Mrs Bolton or Mr Jenkins).

Language

The two sets of prospective grandparents will probably get quite involved in the discussion. They might need calming down. Here are some useful expressions that Mrs Bolton, for instance, can use when talking to her husband:

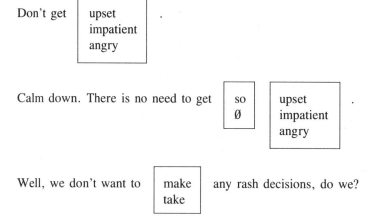

Don't get | upset / impatient / angry | .

Calm down. There is no need to get | so / Ø | upset / impatient / angry | .

Well, we don't want to | make / take | any rash decisions, do we?

See also

EXPRESSING EXASPERATION at not being listened to (pages 71 and 152)
EXPRESSING DISAGREEMENT (pages 150–151)
EXPRESSING DOUBT (pages 149–150)
EXPRESSING INDECISION (page 151)
EXPRESSING OPINIONS (pages 142–143)
EXPRESSING SUGGESTIONS (pages 146–149)
EXPRESSING ALTERNATIVE SUGGESTIONS (pages 146–147)
INTERRUPTING (pages 151–152)
MAKING EVERYBODY ACTIVE (pages 69 and 151–152)

12. IMMORAL CONDUCT? (for groups of 4—5 learners)

Characters

Jane McAdam (a teacher), aged twenty-four. This is her second year at this school. She has spectacular teaching qualifications. She is liked and respected by pupils and colleagues alike. Divorcee. Now pregnant.

Tom Shaw (a pupil), aged eighteen. He has one year until his final exams. He is a very good pupil — intelligent, extremely polite, friendly, gifted. He is liked by pupils and teachers alike.

The story so far

Tom and Jane fell in love with each other last year. Now that Jane is pregnant, they want to live together. Tom's parents are outraged and have appealed to the school to do something about this totally unacceptable situation. They have the support of most of the other parents whose children attend the school.

Setting

The board of directors of the school gathers to discuss the problem. A unanimous decision has to be reached.

> **Lester/Linda Davis.** The situation is disgraceful and both Jane McAdam and Tom Shaw should leave the school immediately. Think of the arguments you are going to use to support your point of view.

> **Bob/Beatrice Pullen.** If a situation like this arises, the teacher is obviously at fault. She should have never allowed herself to get friendly with the pupil in the first place. Tom was seduced and must be protected. Jane McAdam should leave the school. Think of the arguments you are going to use to support your point of view.

Jane/Jack Millington. Something should be done about the present situation. The reputation of the school is most important. It is only because Jane McAdam is obviously an exceptionally good teacher that she should be allowed to stay on. If making Tom Shaw leave the school is the only way of keeping them apart, then that is what should happen. Think of the arguments you are going to use to support your point of view.

Mark/Marjory Patterson. Tom, at eighteen, is responsible for his own actions. He is highly intelligent and the relationship with Mrs McAdam has had no adverse effect on either his or her work. Tom's parents are over-reacting. Tom Shaw and Jane McAdam should both stay at the school and be allowed to live together if that is what they want. Think of the arguments you are going to use to support your point of view.

Eric/Elizabeth Loft. You do not see how anyone can suggest ruining either Tom's or Jane's career because of a personal relationship. It would not be a good idea, though, to let them live together while Tom is still at school. Think of the arguments you are going to use to support your point of view.

Notes

1. In the case of a group of four learners only participating in the role-play, any one of the role-cards can be left out.
2. The role-play lends itself to several optional written follow-up activities. Here are a few examples (learners choose which letter to write):

    (i) One of the directors who took part in the meeting writes a letter to a teacher he or she used to work with, telling her about the meeting and the decision that was taken.

(ii) One of the people involved most directly in the problem (that is, Tom Shaw, Jane McAdam, Mr Shaw or Mrs Shaw) writes a letter to an Agony Aunt describing the situation and asking for advice. This activity can be done in pairs with either Tom and Jane, or Mr Shaw and Mrs Shaw writing one letter.

(iii) The letters writen to an Agony Aunt (see above) can be used for the *Agony Aunt (1)* simulation. Learners should then reply to letters written by other learners (not by themselves).

Language
Making everybody active
What do you think, Mrs Davis?

| Don't |
| Do |

you agree, Miss Pullen?

I don't know what Mr Millington thinks but ...
You're very quiet, Mrs Patterson.

You haven't said | anything / much | so far, Dr Loft.

Let's hear what Mrs Patterson | thinks / says / has to say | .

See also
EXPRESSING DISAGREEMENT IN A DISCUSSION (pages 41 and 148)
THE LANGUAGE OF DISCUSSION (pages 141−152)

13. BREAD (for groups of 3—4 learners)

> **Mother.**   There is no bread in the house. You have a splitting headache. Somebody should go and buy some bread. You are annoyed that nobody has noticed that it is necessary to get some. You start.

> **Father.**   There is no bread in the house. You have recently quarrelled with your girlfriend in the local bakery, so you are trying to avoid the shop. (You cannot say that to anybody, so think of other reasons why you cannot go.)

> **Teenage daughter.**   There is no bread in the house. You think that bread is fattening and that there is always too much of it at home. You do not see why you should go to the bakery if you do not eat any bread.

> **Son, aged five.**   There is no bread in the house. You have found a piece of stale bread put aside for grandma's chickens. You think that if you soak it in milk, it will be delicious. Try to persuade everyone that you are right.

Notes

1. The role of the son is optional.
2. If circumstances demand this, either of the children can be played by learners of the opposite sex.

Language
Expressing exasperation at not being listened to

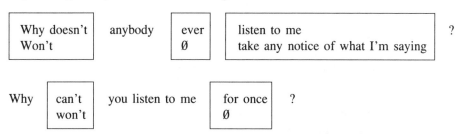

Although *yummy* will probably be the most appropriate word for the five-year-old to use, here are some other adjectives which can describe food that is good to eat:
delicious
exquisite
delightful
mouth-watering
nice
tasty
Here are some words and phrases that might be used by the teenage daughter.
to slim (down)
to lose weight
to diet
to go on a diet
to watch one's weight
to be slim
to put on weight
to gain weight
to be overweight
to be fat, to be plump
This isn't good for you. This is fattening.
eating habits
sensible diet
balanced diet
calorie-controlled diet
vitamins, proteins, calories, carbohydrates

See also
MAKING REQUESTS (pages 128−130)
EXPRESSING INABILITY TO HELP (page 135)
ASKING FOR CLARIFICATION (pages 141−142)
EXPRESSING INDECISION (page 151)
EXPRESSING ALTERNATIVE SUGGESTIONS (pages 146−147)
LODGING COMPLAINTS (in a straightforward way) (page 75)

14. JAM (for groups of 2–3 learners)

> **Paula.** You are fifteen and very much in love. Next Sunday is your boyfriend's birthday and you desperately want to spend the day with him. Your mother is old-fashioned and thinks you are too young to go out with boys, so you cannot tell her why you do not want to stay at home on Sunday. She wants you to help her make strawberry jam. Make your mother change her mind. Tell her, for example, that jam is fattening, or that one should not work on Sundays, or that fruit will be cheaper in two weeks' time. Your godfather is fond of you. Ask him to help you change your mother's mind.

> **Paula's mother.** You want to make strawberry jam next Sunday. You will need Paula's help. You told her so two weeks ago. Now she is telling you she cannot (will not?) help. You do not understand why not. You are suspicious. You never change your mind. Ask Paula's godfather for support.

> **Paula's godfather.** Paula and her mother are arguing. They want you to take sides. You do not care what happens next Sunday. You are in poor health and that is all you are interested in. You keep describing and complaining about your symptoms. (Decide what they are.)

Notes

1. The sex of the participants of the role-play is irrelevant. The teacher will only need to make a few minor changes in the role-cards: Paul might want to meet his girlfriend or Paula might appeal to her godmother for help or Paul's father might want Paul to help him.
2. The role of Paula's godfather is optional.

See

MAKING REQUESTS (pages 128—130)
EXPRESSING INABILITY TO HELP (page 135)
ASKING FOR CLARIFICATION (pages 141—142)
EXPRESSING INDECISION (page 151)
EXPRESSING ALTERNATIVE SUGGESTIONS (pages 146—147)
LODGING COMPLAINTS (in a straightforward way) (page 75)
EXPRESSING EXASPERATION at not being listened to (pages 71 and 152)

*****

15. THE NEIGHBOURS (for groups of three)

Mr/Mrs Mazur. You are a rather old-fashioned, retired lawyer with impeccable manners. You live in the next flat to a very noisy Canadian family (two teenage children and a dog!). In the end you cannot stand it any longer and you decide to go and complain about all the things that annoy you: loud disco music, all-night parties, throwing beer cans out of the windows, dirty staircase (because of the dog), etc. With you is another neighbour, young Krol, the painter. You think one should always be very polite (even when one is making a complaint) and you consider Krol impolite.

Sebastian/Sylvie Krol. You are a young painter. You live in the next flat to a very noisy Canadian family (two teenage children and a dog!). In the end you cannot stand it any longer and you decide to go and complain about all the things that annoy you: loud disco music, all-night parties, racing about in roller skates in front of your door, leaving chewing gum all over the place, etc. With you is another neighbour, old Mr/Mrs Mazur, who is much too polite in your opinion. You do not like people who give preferential treatment to foreigners. You begin.

Tom/Tina Brown.   You are Canadian. You and your family have been living in the country for several months now. You and your spouse travel on business quite a lot and during that time you leave your two teenage children behind. You know that they are very good, quiet children. You do not like the local people very much but you try not to show it. They have a tendency to exaggerate things.

Note
All three roles can be played by both male and female learners.

Language
Lodging complaints (politely)

| I'm very
I'm ever so
I'm
Ø | sorry | to have to say this
to say this
to mention this
to bring this up | but . . . |

| I hate
I don't like | | to have to say this
to say this
to mention this
to bring this up | but . . . |

| I hope you don't mind my
I hate
I don't like
Forgive me for | | saying this
mentioning this
bringing this up | but . . . |

All of the above opening phrases can be followed by a statement of fact and a request, e.g.

'Forgive me for saying this but I have an awful headache, so could you please turn down the radio?'

or by a request only, e.g.

'Forgive me for saying this but could you please turn down the radio?'

Those phrases can also be used for making very polite requests (whith no implication of complaining).

Lodging complaints (in a straightforward way)

I've come to complain about ... (*politely*)

I've just about had enough of this! (*bluntly*)

Why can't you ... | once and for all | ?
                  | Ø |

| Why should I have to |
| I really can't | put up with this any more!
| I won't |
| I don't see why I should |

BE CAREFUL:

Learners should be cautious of giving unintended offence by making blunt complaints.

See also

INTRODUCING ONESELF (page 122)
INTRODUCING SOMEONE (page 123)
RESPONDING after introductions (pages 122–123)
APOLOGISING (before) (page 135)
MAKING REQUESTS (pages 128–130)
ASKING FOR CLARIFICATION (pages 141–142)
GIVING CLARIFICATION (pages 141–142)

16. THE FLAT (for groups of 4—5 learners)

Mrs Bennett has recently been widowed. She has decided that working abroad for a year might help her get over the bereavement. Her contract for the job abroad has just been confirmed and now is the time for the final arrangements. Mrs Bennett has to decide what to do with her flat and asks her children to help her make up her mind.

Tom is a New Zealander. He has been in this country for two years now. Last year he married Eva, Mrs Bennett's eldest daughter.

Marianne is a student in another town. She is living in a hall of residence.

Anna, the youngest, is fourteen. She will go abroad with Mrs Bennett.

> **Mrs Bennett.** You are not used to making decisions. Your late husband used to take care of everything. You miss him so much! You cannot make up your mind. You are inconsistent in what you say. You start the conversation.

> **Eva.** You are rather touchy on the subject of foreigners and their money in case Tom thinks that financial security and creature comforts have been your sole motives in marrying him. You do not mind dropping in at your mother's flat from time to time if it is not rented. Watering plants, however, would require going there rather too frequently.

> **Tom.** You do not understand why your mother-in-law has any scruples about trying to get as much money as possible out of the flat, e.g. by renting it to foreign business people.

> **Anna.** You have mixed feelings about the flat. On the one hand, lots of money is always a good idea, on the other, however, you think that exploiting fellow human beings is contemptible.

> **Marianne.** You are thinking of getting married. (Nobody knows about that yet.) If you do, you will give up your studies and get a job, so your mother's flat would be very useful in the beginning. You have no idea what your mother's reaction will be when she hears about your plans. Tell everybody about your plans only if there is no other way of persuading them that the flat should be left vacant.

Procedure

1. As an optional preliminary activity, learners can discuss what can be done with a vacant flat and what factors should be taken into consideration. If the teacher decides to omit this activity, learners should be presented with the following points for consideration.

(i) Should the flat be rented at all? What are your priorities?
   a. Getting as much money as possible.
   b. Having somebody look after the flat.
   c. Helping somebody in a difficult situation.
   d. Not having problems (and therefore not renting the flat).
   e. Other?

(ii) Who could the flat be rented to?
   a. Somebody you know personally.
   - The rent will have to be nominal only.
   - The flat is not likely to be vandalised.
   - If something is damaged, it will be awkward to ask for reimbursement.
   b. Somebody who has placed an appropriate advertisement in a newspaper.
   - You can get a lot of money.
   - The place may get vandalised.
   - Foreign diplomats or business people are most likely to be well behaved.
   - You can help somebody in need, a single mother or a nurse, for instance.

(iii) Can you think of any alternative solutions?

2. The role-play takes place: the learners decide if Mrs Bennett should or should not rent the flat.

3. If the participants decide that the flat should be rented, the teacher provides the 'Accommodation Wanted' advertisements. The learners choose which one should be answered. If the participants decide otherwise, the teacher suggests consulting the 'Accommodation Wanted' advertisements anyway to see if there are any particularly interesting ones.

Notes

1. The role of Anna is optional.
2. Both Marianne and Anna can be played by male learners, thus becoming Mark and Anthony.

Language
Asking for advice

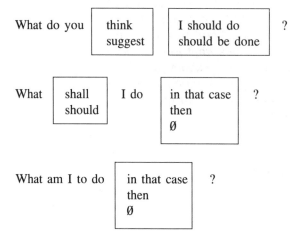

What do you | think / suggest | I should do / should be done | ?

What | shall / should | I do | in that case / then / Ø | ?

What am I to do | in that case / then / Ø | ?

What would you do in my position?

Offering advice
If I were you, I'd ...
Personally, I'd advise you to ...
I think you should ...

Well, you could | always / Ø | ...

See also

17. A HOLIDAY HOME (for pairs of learners)

Judith. Michael, your husband, has just told you that some people both of you know have recently bought a holiday home in the country. Michael has always fancied that idea himself but you think that it does not make any sense at all. Here are some of the arguments you can use. Think of other ones that will support your point of view.

1. A holiday home means spending all your holidays in the same place.
2. Holidays will be just like your everyday life with cooking, washing up and cleaning the place.
3. You will have to buy another refrigerator, washing machine, etc.
4. You will always be worried that the house will be burgled when you are not there.
5. It is crazy to spend a lot of money to buy a place you will use for only one month a year.
6. How will you afford to go to the holiday home if the price of petrol goes up again?

Michael. You have just found out that some people you and Judith, your wife, know have recently bought a holiday home in the country. You have always fancied that idea yourself, so you start talking to Judith about it. She does not seem too keen. You are annoyed that she is always right. Although basically you agree with everything Judith is saying, you do not want to admit that and you contradict all her arguments.

Here are some of the arguments you can use. Think of other ones that will support your point of view.

1. You can afford a holiday home now. Inflation will prevent you from ever again being able to consider the idea of buying one.
2. You will spend the money once and then have so much fun and enjoyment without any additional expenses.

3. You can invite people to stay with you.
4. A house in the country will be paradise for the children.
5. A holiday home is a status symbol.
6. A holiday home is an investment.

Language

Some phrases that can be used in the conversation both by Michael and Judith:

I | take / see | your point but . . .

| Possibly, True, Yes, | but | on the other hand . . . if you look at this from a different point of view . . . looking at this from another point of view . . . |

See also

EXPRESSING OPINIONS (pages 142–143)
EXPRESSING DOUBT (pages 149–150)
EXPRESSING INDECISION (page 151)
DEALING WITH DOUBTS AND OBJECTIONS (page 149)
EXPRESSING ALTERNATIVE SUGGESTIONS (pages 146–147)
EXPRESSING DISAGREEMENT (pages 150–151)

18. SMOKING (for pairs of learners)

A

> Last week you gave up smoking. You are sitting in a restaurant waiting to be served. The woman at the next table is smoking and all the smoke is coming in your direction. She looks rich, arrogant and foreign. You are not in a mood for a quarrel but smoke has really been getting on your nerves lately. You decide to begin a seemingly casual conversation and then, gradually, get round to asking the woman to do something about the cigarette: put it out, hold it in the other hand . . . anything! You begin.

B

> You are a chain-smoker. You are smoking now. You are sitting in a restaurant waiting to be served. The woman at the next table looks very friendly. You feel rather bored and wouldn't mind a chat, especially since you are talkative. You have a tendency to interrupt people before they finish what they are saying. You like telling them your life-story.

Note
The sex of the participants of the role-play is irrelevant.

Language
Some words and phrases connected with smoking:
passive smoking (suffering from inhaling other people's smoke)
to light a cigarette
to put out a cigarette, to stub out a cigarette
ash
ashtray
tobacco
nicotine
tar
matchbox
match
smoking compartment

smoking car, smoking carriage
smoker's cough
lung cancer
stained fingers
health risk
cigarette case
cigarette holder
cigarette lighter
cigarette brand
cigarette end, cigarette butt
chain-smoker
smoker
non-smoker
a filter-tipped cigarette
filter tip
to calm one's nerves
to give up smoking

See also

INTRODUCING ONESELF (page 122)
RESPONDING after introductions (page 122)
TALKING ABOUT THE WEATHER (pages 83—84 and 133)
TALKING ABOUT LIKES AND DISLIKES (pages 62—64 and 123—125)
ASKING FOR OPINIONS (pages 142—144)
ASKING ABOUT PLANS (pages 126—127)
RESPONDING to the above (pages 126—127)
OFFERING HELP (page 134)
REJECTING AN OFFER OF HELP (page 134)
EXTENDING AN INVITATION (page 140)
REFUSING AN INVITATION (page 141)
PAYING COMPLIMENTS (page 130)
RESPONDING to compliments (page 130)
APOLOGISING (before) (page 135)
MAKING REQUESTS (pages 128—130)
INTERRUPTING (pages 151—152)
LODGING COMPLAINTS (politely) (pages 74 and 153)

19. ON THE TRAIN (for pairs of learners)

The two participants of this role-play are the only passengers in a train compartment.

A

> You love speaking English. You also love to talk and to find out everything about other people, even if this means asking very personal questions. What is wrong with personal questions, anyway? Try to find out as much as possible about the other passenger, who must be English (you have seen the name-tag on the suitcase).

B

> You are Scots (a Scottish nationalist, as a matter of fact). You dislike talking about yourself but you hate being rude, so you can never tell anybody to mind their own business. Say as little about yourself as possible. Be evasive. Try to divert the other person's attention. (You have reserved your seat, so you cannot leave the compartment!)

Language
Instead of answering personal questions, B might try to discuss the weather.

Talking about the weather

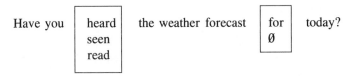

It looks like rain, doesn't it?
Looks a bit like rain, doesn't it?
I suppose it'll clear up later.
Isn't it awful today?

What a	chilly		day		!
	freezing		morning		
	lovely		afternoon		
	marvellous		evening		
	rainy		night		
	terrible				

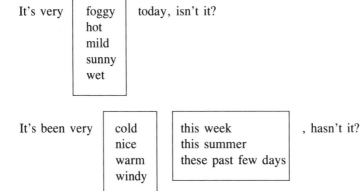

It's very | foggy | today, isn't it?
hot
mild
sunny
wet

It's been very | cold | this week | , hasn't it?
nice | this summer
warm | these past few days
windy

See also

INTRODUCING ONESELF (page 122)
RESPONDING after introductions (page 122)
TALKING ABOUT LIKES AND DISLIKES (pages 62—64 and 123—125)
ASKING FOR OPINIONS (pages 142—144)
ASKING ABOUT PLANS (pages 126—127)
RESPONDING to the above (pages 126—127)
ASKING ABOUT PLANS AND REPLYING EVASIVELY (page 58)
OFFERING HELP (page 134)
REJECTING AN OFFER OF HELP (page 134)
EXTENDING AN INVITATION (page 140)
REFUSING AN INVITATION (page 141)
STALLING FOR TIME (pages 32 and 154)
REFUSING TO ANSWER A QUESTION (pages 32 and 155)

*****

20. THE ONCE-IN-A-LIFETIME HOLIDAY (for groups of 3—4 learners)

Mr Notkin. You have retired. For the past ten years you and your wife have been spending rather uneventful holidays at the seaside. You have recently met two foreigners. They want to sell you tickets for a cruise around the world. You think that their suggestion is very interesting, especially as they say you will get a discount if you pay immediately in your own currency in cash. Ask for as many details as possible (the exact prices, dates, conditions, etc.). Try to convince your wife that both of you deserve some fun.

Mrs Notkin. You have retired. For the past ten years you and your husband have been spending rather uneventful holidays at the seaside. You have recently met two foreigners. They want to sell you tickets for a cruise around the world. You think that their suggestion is very interesting but you are slightly suspicious too. Those people are asking for a lot of money! Ask all sorts of questions (including the same ones twice!) to check if they are telling the truth. You think that your husband wants to spend your lifetime's savings too easily.

Barry/Barbara Baker. You are pretending to be a foreigner. Your real name is Piekarczyk. You desperately need a lot of money. You are even ready to steal it from the retired couple you have recently met. You want to 'sell' them bogus tickets for a cruise around the world. Tell them all the details and point out that your offer is a bargain (discount for immediate payment in local currency, cash, etc.). You think that your partner is no good at lying. Try to do all the talking.

Mike/Milly Smith. You are pretending to be a foreigner. Your real name is Kowal. You desperately need a lot of money. You are even ready to steal it from the retired couple you have recently met. You want to 'sell' them bogus tickets for a cruise around the world. Tell them all the details and point out that your offer is a bargain (discount for immediate payment in local currency, cash, etc.). You think that your partner is no good at lying. Try to do all the talking.

Note

The role of Smith is optional.

Language

Here is what Mr Notkin might say:

Well, all this certainly sounds like a marvellous idea, wouldn't you say so, dear?

That offer is definitely worth considering.

Surely it wouldn't be wise to miss an opportunity like this!

Think of all the exotic places we would see.

I've always wanted to travel . . .

| We could have a | second honeymoon, dear. |
| This could be our | |

Here are some of the objections that Mrs Notkin might raise:

That's all very well, but will we be insured?

Can we be sure that the accommodation will be comfortable?

What will happen if the cruise is cancelled at the last moment?

All this sounds like a real bargain and that's precisely what makes it so suspicious.

That's all true, I suppose, but can we really afford a holiday like that?

I'm not sure we should spend so much money on a holiday, dear.

Baker and Smith might reply:

We can assure you that everything will be taken care of.

| You needn't worry about | anything | . |
| | a thing | |

| This may seem | impossible | but you can pay less by paying cash now. |
| | strange to you | |

You wouldn't really want to miss a bargain like that, would you?

There is no need to worry about any arrangements; everything will be taken care of.

See also

EXPRESSING DOUBT (pages 149—150)
EXPRESSING INDECISION (page 151)
DEALING WITH DOUBTS AND OBJECTIONS (page 149)
OFFERING ADVICE (pages 78 and 127)
EXPRESSING TENTATIVE AGREEMENT (page 147)

B. SIMULATIONS

Remember, in simulations the learners are told who they are, but express their own opinions.

21. A SCHOOL COMMITTEE (for groups of 3−5 learners)

The situation
You are on a committee which is to decide on the subjects teenagers should be taught in a secondary school.

All children in the whole country get the same schooling. They spend seven years in a primary school (age 6−13) and then go to a secondary school, where they stay for the next four years, until they are seventeen. Then they have the choice of either going to work or to a university. Even though this system is far from ideal, nothing can be done about it at the moment. The committee can only try to improve it by working out a sensible balance of subjects the pupils will take. You have *carte blanche*, as long as the pupils spend thirty hours a week at school and no more than 20 per cent of the subjects are available as options. Not all subjects have to be academic. You can include cooking, gardening, woodwork, etc.

Procedure
1. Learners prepare the curriculum in groups of 3−5. A strict time-limit is given ('If your reports do not reach the Ministry on time, they will not be taken into consideration').
2. New groups are formed. Their size will depend on the original number of groups, since in each new group there will be one member of all the previous groups. Learners inform one another about the curriculums they have prepared.

   Example of mixing groups (twelve learners)

Stage 1

Stage 2

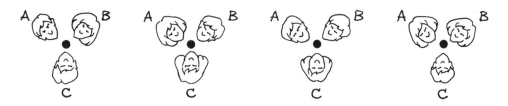

3. (*optional*) Learners go back to their original groups and discuss the other proposals. They decide if they want to make any changes. Rather than exchange information, learners compare their opinions. They all listened to the same reports, after all, even if presented by various people.

Language

Some of the possible components of the curriculum:

1. Architecture	11. Music
2. Art	12. Nature Study
3. Computers	13. Physical Education
4. Cooking	14. Political Sciences
5. Craft	15. Psychology
6. Domestic Science	16. Religious Education
7. Drama	17. Sewing
8. Economics	18. Sex Education
9. Gardening	19. Social Sciences
10. Human Geography	20. Woodwork

The following distinctions may be helpful:

curriculum/ kəˈrɪkjʊləm / (plural: curriculums or curricula) — subjects covered by a course of study in a school, college, etc. (e.g. geography, history).

syllabus/ ˈsɪləbəs / (plural: syllabuses or syllabi) — outline or itemised summary of the contents of a course of studies; programme of studies within a subject (e.g. mountain formation, South America, rainfall; eighteenth-century Europe, nineteenth-century China).

See also

MAKING EVERYBODY ACTIVE (pages 69 and 151−152)
THE LANGUAGE OF DISCUSSION (pages 141−152)

22. ARE YOU HONEST? (for groups of 4−5 learners)

You live in an imaginary society where at the end of the year a special board evaluates people's honesty. As members of that board you and your friends are to evaluate the following people on a 1−10 scale, 1 point being given to a perfectly honest person, 10 to somebody who has committed a very serious offence. Unfortunately, no additional information is available.

---

1. A student studying for a very important examination tears out a few pages from a library book. He needs them very badly and the book is rarely used by others.
2. Another student studying for a very important examination marks pages of a library book with a pen.
3. A journalist needs a specialised atlas for his work. Such atlases are not available in shops, so he borrows one from a library, says he has lost it and pays for it.
4. A young woman avoids paying her bus fare. She thinks the bus service is bad.
5. A young man buys a cheap ticket to the cinema and sits in a more expensive seat, since one is available.
6. A research worker wants to get a scholarship to France. All the candidates must take an examination in French. He is afraid he will not pass it, so a friend who speaks very good French takes the examination for him.
7. A worker at a shampoo factory regularly smuggles out shampoo for himself and his family.
8. New lamps have been bought for a hotel. A man who works in the hotel changes his own old lamp for a new one which he takes home.
9. An unknown artist imitates the style of a famous painter and in this way sells his pictures to private collectors.
10. An academic publishes falsified results of an experiment.

Here is another list as an alternative or for a further simulation.

---

1. A well-educated engineer (his education was free, he also received a grant during his studies) works as an unskilled labourer (he earns more money this way).
2. A shop assistant needs money desperately. He takes it from the shop and, unnoticed, returns it next day.
3. A man wants time off work to redecorate his flat, so he goes to a doctor and asks for a sickness certificate saying he is ill. He is given one.
4. An academic asks a colleague to read his manuscript. He is then killed in a car crash. The colleague publishes the manuscript as his own.
5. Two academics work on a manuscript. Then one of them is killed in a car crash. The other publishes the manuscript as his own.
6. A coach driver on a long-distance coach is paid a fare by a passenger who does not insist on getting a ticket. The driver puts the money in his pocket.

7. A man sends a unjustified anonymous letter, as a result of which a good specialist loses his job.
8. A nurse takes a packet of cotton-wool from the hospital where she works.
9. A nurse takes a packet of cotton-wool from a self-service shop.
10. A well-off family decides to send their eighty-year-old grandmother to an old people's home.

Notes

1. Learners work in groups of 4—5. The results arrived at by the various groups can be compared and followed by a general discussion.
2. Learners can be asked to compile their own lists of ethically dubious cases.
3. Any of the suggested cases can be chosen as a subject for a discussion. 'Should the person involved be punished and, if so, how?' (see *Punishment*). Alternatively, learners are told whether they are to be for or against punishment (see *Agree!*).

Language

The following vocabulary items may be needed in the discussion. (The definitions come from the *Oxford Advanced Learner's Dictionary of Current English*, third edition, 1974.)

crime — offence for which there is severe punishment by law.

felony — major serious crime, e.g. murder, armed robbery, arson.

misdemeanour/ ˌmɪsdɪˈmiːnə(r) / — offence less serious than a felony.

offence — crime, sin, breaking of a rule.

petty (as in petty crime) — small, unimportant.

BE CAREFUL:

The correct phrases are: commit a crime, commit murder.

See also

EXPRESSING SUPPOSITION (pages 40 and 156)
MAKING EVERYBODY ACTIVE (pages 69 and 151—152)
THE LANGUAGE OF DISCUSSION (pages 141—152)

23. BABY GIRL FOR ADOPTION (for groups of 4—5 learners)

You are on an adoption committee and your task is to select a family for a baby girl. Here are the candidates:

Mr and Mrs Thompson. She is twenty-seven and a telephonist. He is a thirty-year-old bus driver. Average income. They cannot have children. Both would prefer a boy but as they have been waiting for a baby for a very long time, they are prepared to adopt a girl.
Mr and Mrs Green. Both are thirty-one and doctors. They have been married for seven years. They can have children of their own but feel that the world is overpopulated as it is.
Mr and Mrs Hill. A teacher aged twenty-four and an engineer aged twenty-five. They have a five-year-old son and very much want a girl. Doctors say that it would be dangerous for Mrs Hill to give birth to another baby.
Miss Wilson. She is forty and works as a cleaner in a kindergarten. She comes from a big family. She has never been married and has always dreamt of having a daughter.
Mrs Diggs. She is a thirty-five-year-old divorced nurse. She had a child of her own, who died.

Procedure
1. Learners work in groups of 4—5. They decide who should adopt the baby girl.

2. Depending on the decision the learners arrive at, one of the following letters to the adoption committee is given to them. The groups then discuss the problem of how tragedies like that can be avoided, what advice should be given, what factors adoption committees should take into consideration, etc.

The letter for learners who have selected the Thompsons, the Greens or the Hills:

```
Dear Adoption Committee,
We were very happily married for several years until we adopted a
child and from then on things have gone from bad to worse.  From
the beginning I have never had any feeling for the child.  I should
never have listened to all the friends and relatives who told me
that I would learn to love her.  I should have followed my instinct
and sent her back before it was too late (she is five now).  I did
not seriously consider that possibility then because my husband
loved her so much from the beginning.  I feel lonely and guilty.  I
tried so hard to love the girl but I can't.  My husband hates me
for this.  I really don't know what to do.  Please help me.
```

The letter for learners who have selected Miss Wilson or Mrs Diggs:

```
Dear Adoption Committee,
For many years I wanted to have a child.  Finally I adopted a baby
girl and from then on things have gone from bad to worse.  From
the beginning I have never had any feeling for the child.  I should
never have listened to all the friends and relatives who told me
that I would learn to love her.  I should have followed my instinct
and sent her back before it was too late (she is five now).  I feel
lonely and guilty.  I tried so hard to love the girl but I can't.
I really don't know what to do.  Please help me.
```

Language
See
STALLING FOR TIME (pages 32 and 154)
EXPRESSING DISAGREEMENT IN A DISCUSSION (pages 41 and 148)
MAKING EVERYBODY ACTIVE (pages 69 and 151−152)
THE LANGUAGE OF DISCUSSION (pages 141−152)

*****

24. KOWALSKI (for groups of 2−4 learners)

You can use this simulation as it is with the setting 'Poland', or you can set it in your
own country and for the name 'Kowalski', substitute a name from your country. The
reunion is then of expatriates of the name you have chosen, returning to your country.

You are one of the couriers at the Annual Kowalski Reunion — a meeting of the Kowalskis
who live outside Poland. You have just found out that on top of the usual duties of a courier,
basically those of a troubleshooter, you have to plan a five-day tour of Poland for the
ten people you will be responsible for. One of the other couriers, who have to prepare
itineraries too, has suggested holding a brainstorming session.

Here are some of the problems you have to bear in mind:

1. The age of the participants of the reunion ranges from eighteen to sixty-five.
2. For some of them this will be the first visit to the old country; others come here almost
    every other year.
3. Some Kowalskis speak Polish, others do not. All of them speak English, though.
4. They come from all walks of life.
5. The groups of ten have been formed at random according to the hotels the participants
    of the Reunion will be staying at.

The organisers of the reunion have assured you that the cost of the trip is irrelevant. Also, in spite of the fact that this is the height of the tourist season, there will not be any problems with either transport or accommodation. All the necessary arrangements will be taken care of.

Notes
1. The learners should work in small groups.
2. It is possible to conduct the activity using the pyramid discusion format (see *Procedure* in Part One). Individual learners select, for instance, the five places the Kowalskis should see in Poland. They then compare their choices in pairs, agree on one list, get into groups of four, etc.
3. Instead of deciding which places in Poland the Kowalskis should be taken to, learners can consider which three sights or places of interest in their town or in their area would be worth showing to the visitors.

Language
Some useful words and phrases:
tour, to tour, tourist
visit, to visit, visitor
to go sightseeing
itinerary
route
timetable
guide
courier
gallery, art gallery, picture gallery
collection, exhibition, museum
palace, castle, manor house
monument
sight
place of interest
painting, sculpture, tapestry

BE CAREFUL:
A person who works for a travel agency and who accompanies tourists is called a *courier*.

See also
ASKING FOR ADVICE (pages 78 and 127—128)
TALKING ABOUT LIKES AND DISLIKES (pages 62—64 and 123—125)
MAKING EVERYBODY ACTIVE (pages 69 and 151—152)
THE LANGUAGE OF DISCUSSION (pages 141—152)

25. AN AD CAMPAIGN (for groups of 3—4 learners)

You work in the publicity department of a company that is about to launch a new brand of soap. The company is in rather bad financial shape and you know that if this advertising campaign does not work and the product does not sell, all the people in your department (including yourself) will be fired. Your department's task is to think of a name for the new brand and a slogan to go with it, as well as to suggest a few ideas for magazine advertisements, radio and television commercials, etc. The company hopes to export the new soap, so the campaign should be conducted in English. Explain the situation to the others in the department.

Notes
1. (optional) Having designed the campaign, learners write a short item for the company newspaper, in which they explain what the advertising campaign will be like.
2. The teacher can choose a different product to be brought onto the market, e.g. a television set, an alarm clock, a chocolate bar.

Language
Advertisements are used
   to promote a new product,
   to market a product,
   to persuade people to buy a product,
   to make an impact on people.
Advertisements should be
   appealing,
   attractive,
   eye-catching.
An advertisement on the radio or television is called a commercial.

See also
TALKING ABOUT LIKES AND DISLIKES (pages 62—64 and 123—125)
ASKING FOR ADVICE (pages 78 and 127—128)
EXPRESSING INABILITY TO HELP (page 135)
PAYING COMPLIMENTS (page 130)
RESPONDING TO COMPLIMENTS (page 130)
MAKING EVERYBODY ACTIVE (pages 69 and 151—152)
THE LANGUAGE OF DISCUSSION (pages 141—152)

26. PET HATE (for groups of 3—5 learners)

A monthly magazine called *Nowadays* has a regular competition for the 'Pet Hate' letter of the month. Readers write about the things they dislike most and which keep annoying them. Every month a jury chooses the letter of the month. Its author receives a year's free subscription to *Nowadays*. Once a year a special jury is appointed. Its task is to select the 'Pet Hate' letter of the year. The winner receives a lifelong subscription to the magazine.

The learners, divided into groups of about four, are appointed as the special jury. They decide what criteria they will be guided by. Will they look for letters that are most sensible, most naive, most unexpected, most amusing? Each jury is then provided with twelve letters, from which one has to be chosen.

Letters

```
Dear Nowadays,
Don't people who write horoscopes realise what a grave
responsibility they are accepting in return for the money they earn
in this shameful way?  A dear friend of mine has recently put
himself in an unscrupulous horoscope writer's hands.  He went along
with his horoscope which instructed him to change his life-style
completely.  I won't go into the painful details; let me just say
that he has made a lot of people very unhappy in the process.
Pseudo-astrologers should be banned!
Unhappily,

Nora Jackson
West Midlands
```

```
Dear 'Pet Hate',
Why don't shampoo bottles have smaller holes in the top?  Is this a
way of making us buy more?  It makes me shudder to see how much
is wasted by accidently pouring too much!
Yours, hating waste,

                              Terry Hott
                              Norwich
```

```
Dear Sir,
I would like to protest strongly against people who issue invitations
to pop round to see them but don't bother to turn the television off
while you are there.
                         Yours faithfully,

                         Roy Brooke
                         Grampian
```

Dear Nowadays,
I fail to understand why all airlines have a set luggage allowance of
20 kg irrespective of the traveller's body weight. I weigh about
51 kg and quite often have to pay for my excess luggage. Other
people may weigh anything up to 120 kg but they have the same
20 kg allowance. Perhaps on buying a ticket one should be asked
how much one weighs and then allocated a baggage allowance
accordingly. Surely that would be fairer than the present system!
                                              Yours lightly,

                                    Nancy Coleman
                                    Coleraine

Dear Sir/Madam,
What do those supposedly loving mothers think they are doing? I'm
appalled by the vast number of mums whose first action on picking
up a tot who has tripped up is ... to spank him. Don't they
realise that the child is already in pain? What's more, when
challenged those mothers claim it's all for the child's good.
Yours faithfully,

Derek Duff
Cambridge

Dear Letters Page,
When I ask a hairdresser how long I'll have to wait before I can
have my hair done, I invariably hear 'Just a few minutes, dear'.
It can then take anything up to three hours! Exactly the same
thing happens even if I have made an appointment. Why can't
hairdressers respect the fact that some of us have better things to
do than sit about for three hours doing nothing?
                                              Yours,

                                    Denise Quirk
                                    Exeter

Dear Editor,
I protest against receiving private telephone calls during my office
hours! True, I don't have a telephone at home but what's wrong
with dropping in to see me or sending a letter? My friends don't
seem to realise that I go to work in order to work and not to chat
to them. When I tell them I'm busy, they don't take me seriously.
'Surely you don't work a full eight hours a day,' they say
incredulously. What's wrong with wanting to work in one's working
time, I'd like to ask!
Yours, writing in my own time,

                                    Mary Broom
                                    Croydon

Dear Letters,
My pet hate is a toilet roll which is glued through about six layers
of paper before you reach a smooth beginning. Isn't that a
disgraceful waste?

                         Yours now with scissors,

                         Allan Kay
                         Glasgow

Dear Pet Hates,
Why do all pushchairs face the wrong way? I'm sure my baby
would prefer to look at me and feel safe than to look at the
crowded streets, full of aggressive people.
Yours faithfully

Keith Horton
London

Dear Pet Hates,
Where has all the glue on stamps gone? Every time I buy a stamp
at a post office, I have to ask for some glue since this is the only
way to persuade a stamp to stay on the envelope! By paying for
the stamp, aren't we paying for the glue too?
Yours ever,

Don Cottle
Northants

Dear Editor,
Why can't bottle tops fit properly? I'm fed up with buying fizzy
drinks that have lost their fizz!
                       Yours annoyedly,

                       David Felton
                       Tyneside

Dear Letters Page,
Why can't fashion designers bring back the side zip in trousers? I
am a woman and I don't see any need for a zip in the front.
Besides, one at the side is so much more becoming.
Yours faithfully,

Shirley Grey
Swansea

Notes

1. The special jury may decide to select two runners-up.
2. Learners compare the choices they made in different groups.

Alternative procedure

1. Learners write their own Pet Hate letters. This can be preceded by reading a few (or indeed all) of the twelve letters that are provided and/or a general discussion. The actual writing may be set as homework. If it is done in class, however, learners can work in pairs. The letters should be written on separate pieces of paper and properly addressed.
2. Learners are divided into groups of about four and are given another group's letters. This arrangement is meant to prevent the learners having to judge their own entries. The learners then select the Pet Hate letter of the month.

Language

When discussing the Pet Hate letters, learners might use some of the following words:

This is a/an

basic	issue
complex	matter
complicated	problem
crucial	question
difficult	
fundamental	
great	
important	
major	
serious	
significant	
common	
commonplace	
everyday	
familiar	
insignificant	
minor	
ordinary	
simple	
trivial	
unimportant	
extraordinary	
odd	
peculiar	
remarkable	
strange	

See also
MAKING EVERYBODY ACTIVE (pages 69 and 151—152)
THE LANGUAGE OF DISCUSSION (pages 141—152)

*****

27. AGONY AUNT (1) (for groups of 2—3 learners)

You and your friends have a part-time job as Agony Aunt 'Sandy' in a popular women's magazine. Now all of you are working on a reply to one of the following letters.

```
Dear Sandy,
I am sixteen and have never had a steady boyfriend.  I am
desperate to go out with Norman, but I can't get him to ask me.
It's no use telling me to give up, because I am crazy about him and
will try anything.  Please, please suggest something.
It is not the way I look, because I'm sure I'm attractive.  I'd
really like to marry and have a family.  I'm terrified I'll end up
an old maid like an aunt of mine.  A cousin used to tease me about
ending up like her.  It upset me at the time, and now I think it'll
probably come true.  What can I do?
                                        Yours,

                                        Alison
```

```
Dear Sandy,
I'm a married woman, no longer young but very much in love with
another man.  Both our marriages are sadly lacking.  Although my
husband loves me, I have hardly been able to return that love, and
only my children have given me any real happiness, so when they
grew up and left home, there was nothing left.  The man I love
doesn't love his wife, but would never leave her.  When my
husband learnt about the situation, the relationship had to end.
Although this was some years ago now, my feelings for this other
man have never changed.  Am I being unfair staying with my
husband who knows I'm unable to give him the love he wants so
much?  Should I leave him and try to make a new life on my own?
Whatever I decide, it's not going to make my husband any happier
and I shall never be happy myself.  What do you think I should do?
Yours sincerely,

Beth
```

Dear 'Sandy',
The woman I love lives about 200 kilometres away from me. I've
known her for nearly two years and we see each other about one
weekend in three. She tells me that there is something she's
sorting out, and she can't tell me more about herself until she's
sure. I've never even met her family. This is all so stupid.
Sometimes I feel like never seeing her again, but I'm so curious to
know why, whenever I ask about her family, or where she lives,
she avoids the question and tells me to be patient. I'm sure she's
not married. When I'm with her I trust her, but when I'm not - I
have doubts. What's your advice?

                                         Yours confused,

                                         Chris

Dear Sandy,
Life is so awful that I just don't know what to do. I've never had
any boyfriends. My job has always been boring - just typing.
Nothing has ever been right at home or at school. I'm forty now
and am sure I'll never succeed at anything. When a woman is
beautiful everything is OK; when she's plain, nobody notices her.
Doctors just give me sedatives. I've failed at suicide twice just as
I have failed at everything else. Please help, even if it is only to
agree that some of us can never be happy.
Yours desperately,

Dorothy

Notes
1. Learners work in small groups of two or three.
2. After the letters have been replied to, groups that had the same letters compare their answers.

Language
'Agony Aunt' is a colloquial name for a personal advice columnist, that is, a journalist who replies to letters from people with personal problems. The two most famous American Agony Aunts are Ann Landers and Abigail Van Buren, better known as 'Dear Abby'.

BE CAREFUL:
The correct pronunciation of 'aunt' is |ɑ:nt|

See also
ASKING FOR ADVICE (pages 78 and 127–128)
OFFERING ADVICE (pages 78 and 127)
EXPRESSING SUPPOSITION (pages 40 and 156)
THE LANGUAGE OF DISCUSSION (pages 141–152)

28. PRANKSTERS (for groups of 2−3 learners)

You are a teenager who likes to play jokes on people. You decide to write a reply to one of the following 'Situations Wanted' advertisements. Ask your friends to help you.

Energetic translator (English, German) wants interesting and challenging work. Fed up with technical translations. Willing to work on novels, poems, etc from home. Box 476.

Experienced travelling companion will arrange your business trip/world tour so that everything runs as smoothly as possible. Write with proposed itinerary and I will reply with outline plans and prices. Box 524.

I'm prepared to put money and my management expertise into your unusual idea for international export. Any geniuses or inventors out there? Write a brief proposal in confidence. Box 485.

Note
Learners can decide for themselves which classified advertisement they wish to answer.

Language
See
THE LANGUAGE OF DISCUSSION (pages 141−152)

* * * * *

29. AGENTS (for groups of 2−3 learners)

You are a counter-intelligence officer whose task is to expose a network of foreign agents, which has begun to operate in your country. You have just been given a telegram that was intercepted a few days ago, as well as fourteen pieces of torn paper (see next page). There are reasons to believe that at least some of the scraps, found in room 403 by a chambermaid, are indeed the coded letter referred to in the telegram. Unfortunately, the rest of the letter (or perhaps letters) was destroyed beyond recognition.

Try to reconstruct the crucial letter filling in the gaps. Work out at least one hypothesis as to what the coded message could be. Ask your colleagues to help you.

```
TELEGRAM   TELEGRAM   TELEGRAM   TELEGRAM   TELEGRAM

SANDY  LANE

EUROPE  HOTEL  RM  403

CONTINUE  DAILY  NOON  CALLS  EXPECT  LETTER  USUAL

CODE  FOLLOWED  IAN

   TELEGRAM   TELEGRAM   TELEGRAM   TELEGRAM   TELEGRAM
```

Dolores can walk after all.

As far as my lodgings are concerned, I'm not allowed to sneeze
(let alone use my hairdryer) without my landlady's prior consent.

Getting buttons to match was such a bother.

I'm all calm and relaxed and leave him more or less to his own devices.

Did Pete say what he wanted?

I'm meeting them at 7.

Friday morning

Dear Sandy
I'll have to type this, you understand.

Our bilateral contacts have suffered a severe setback.

I got a letter from Crete. You know, the one I've been waiting for.
No news yet, however. Why, I keep asking myself.

He asked me to send it to her. Like hell I will.

Hi,
      I'm sorry this will reach you so late.

I suppose I'll have to get some. The problem is in choosing the
right colour. How am I to know what he likes?

I fail to understand why she demands a fee. Isn't personal
satisfaction more important?

The aeroplane was delayed by about six and a half hours.

Notes

1. Learners can compare their hypotheses.
2. Copying the fragments onto separate pieces of paper will help the learners in their guesswork.
3. A good deal of imagination is indispensable in this activity.

See

EXPRESSING SUPPOSITION (pages 40 and 156)
THE LANGUAGE OF DISCUSSION (pages 141–152)

30. 'C' (1) (for groups of 2–3 learners)

A new department store called 'C' will open next month. The following competition is part of an extensive advertising campaign launched on this occasion. You and your friends have decided to take part in it.

Answer the following questions and then tell us in no more than twenty witty words why 'C' is the most interesting letter in the alphabet. Send your entry on a postcard to reach us not later than the end of the month and maybe *you* will be the winner of our 'C'pecial offer!

1. What sort of clothes do people on catwalks wear?
2. What does one use a centavo for?
3. Which of the following can be cerulean?
   a. earth   b. mountains   c. sea   d. air
4. Where are you most likely to find a celandine?
5. Who uses catheters?

Remember that our 'C'pecial offer is waiting for you!

Procedure
1. If no dictionaries can be provided during the activity, learners can be asked to find out at home the meaning of the following words: *catwalk, centavo, cerulean, celandine, catheter*. No context should be given.
2. Learners work on the competition.
3. The competition entries are judged by groups of learners. The best one in each group is chosen. Groups should be arranged in such a way that learners do not assess their own entries.

Note
This is not a vocabulary exercise. The words have been chosen for their relative obscurity and need not become part of the learners' vocabulary. *'C' (2)* is an easier version of this activity.

Answers

1. Fashionable clothes or work clothes: catwalk is a platform for a fashion show.
2. For paying: a centavo is a Latin American coin.
3. Sea: cerulean is a shade of blue.
4. In a garden or in a field: a celandine is a small yellow wild flower.
5. Surgeons: a catheter is a surgical tube.

Language
Asking about the meaning of a word

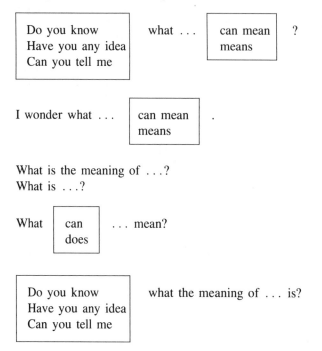

See also
EXPRESSING INABILITY TO HELP (page 135)
RESPONDING to the above (page 135)
EXPRESSING SUPPOSITION (pages 40 and 156)
MAKING EVERYBODY ACTIVE (pages 69 and 151−152)
THE LANGUAGE OF DISCUSSION (pages 141−152)

31. 'C' (2) (for groups of 2–3 learners)

A new department store called 'C' will open next month. The following competition is part of an extensive advertising campaign launched on this occasion. You and your friends have decided to take part in it.

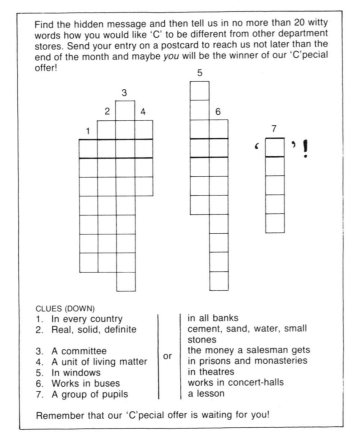

Find the hidden message and then tell us in no more than 20 witty words how you would like 'C' to be different from other department stores. Send your entry on a postcard to reach us not later than the end of the month and maybe *you* will be the winner of our 'C'pecial offer!

CLUES (DOWN)
1. In every country
2. Real, solid, definite
3. A committee
4. A unit of living matter
5. In windows
6. Works in buses
7. A group of pupils

or

in all banks
cement, sand, water, small stones
the money a salesman gets
in prisons and monasteries
in theatres
works in concert-halls
a lesson

Remember that our 'C'pecial offer is waiting for you!

Note

After the competition entries have been prepared, they are judged by groups of learners. The best one in each group is chosen. Groups should be arranged in such a way that learners do not assess their own entries.

Answers

1. *Capital*
2. *Concrete*
3. *Commission*
4. *Cell*
5. *Curtain*
6. *Conductor*
7. *Class*

The hidden message: Come to 'C'!

Language
Some of the questions that can be asked when solving a crossword puzzle:
What is 3 down?

| Do you know | what 3 down is? |
| I wonder | |

Have you any idea what 4 across is?

See also
EXPRESSING INABILITY TO HELP (page 135)
RESPONDING to the above (page 135)
EXPRESSING SUPPOSITION (pages 40 and 156)
MAKING EVERYBODY ACTIVE (pages 69 and 151—152)
THE LANGUAGE OF DISCUSSION (pages 141—152)

C. DISCUSSIONS

Remember, in discussions each learner is himself and expresses his own opinion (except where the activity asks the learners to express opinions opposite to their own for the experience of arguing another point of view).

32. IAN (for groups of 2—3 learners)

Procedure
1. Give each pair a copy of half of the letter opposite. They must try to reconstruct the missing part of the letter. Some work on part A, others on part B. If there is an odd number of learners (or if the number of pairs is not even), some learners can work in groups of three.
2. Learners compare the results of their efforts with those of another pair who have been working on the *same* part of the letter. Together they try to establish the context in which the letter had been written. Here are some of the questions that can be asked:

  ● Who wrote the letter? Who is Ian?
  ● Who is the letter addressed to?
  ● Why was it written?

19th May

Ma chère

   Well, here is what happened. On Saturday I had a taxi
booked for 5.15 a.m. It didn't arrive because, as it turned out
later, the taxi people put it down for 5.15 p.m. Minor difference,
you'll no doubt agree. I had to call them, which wasn't all that
simple, since there was no phone in the house. In the end the
taxi turned up and I managed to get away from that god-forsaken
village to the railway station just in time to catch the 5.47 to
London. It was supposed to arrive at 7.14 but was 15 min
late, needless to say. Can't those trains ever be
goodness sake? Even getting the tube that day
than usual. I'll spare you the details tho

   The coach was to leave at 8 sharp
minutes to get to the meeting place
wouldn't wait for me - why shou   utes
imagine how fast I would've   on time, for
Ridiculous, considering t   was more difficult
didn't leave till half   ugh.
but somehow one rare
      We   , so I had exactly 4
                           There was no doubt they
                      ld they, after all? - so can you
                     had to run? Instead I took a taxi.
                    he distance and the fact that the coach
                   past. I suppose I could've expected that
                  ly assumes that things won't work ...
            got on the ferry at Dover and I immediately regretted
my decision. What an absurd idea that was! I felt like going home
at once. I couldn't though, could I? Unless I fancied a long swim.
I felt so depressed I even persuaded myself to chat up a girl to
keep myself amused.

   We got to our destination at 1 a.m. and sure enough there was a
problem with our hotel reservations. I'll tell you all about those
some other time, otherwise I'll never get this letter posted.
I'll send you a telegram as soon as I hear from Crete.

   Look after yourself, Liebchen, and don't try to be too brave.

                                              Ian

3. Those learners who have been working on part A are joined by those who have been working on part B. They compare the different ways in which the letter was reconstructed in stages 1 and 2 and the different interpretations that were suggested. The above procedure is similar to that of a pyramid discussion (see *Procedure* in Part One) and can be illustrated as follows: (The desks are shown in a long row only for the convenience of the diagram.)

Stage 1

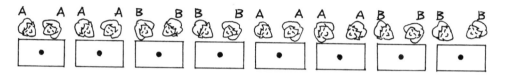

Stage 2

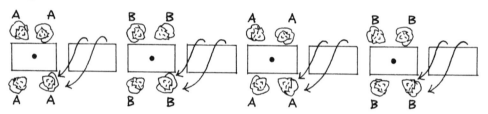

Stage 3

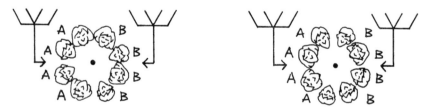

Alternative procedure

1. Pairs of learners try to reconstruct the missing part of the letter.
2. Learners compare the results of their efforts with those of another pair who have been working on the other part of the letter. Together they try to establish the context in which the letter had been written.
3. (optional) Learners who have been working in different pairs compare the ways they reconstructed the letter and the answers they arrived at.

Stage 1

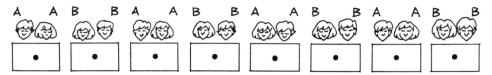

Stage 2 (optional)

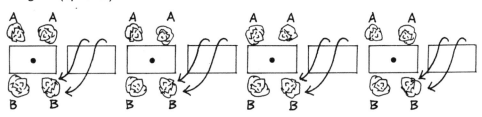

Stage 3

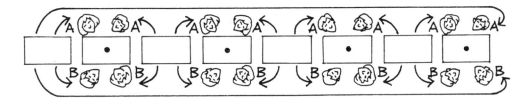

Note

Working with part B of the letter is much more difficult than with Part A.

Language

BE CAREFUL:

Ian is pronounced |ɪən| or |iːən|.

See also

ASKING ABOUT THE MEANING OF A WORD (pages 104 and 131)
EXPRESSING SUPPOSITION (pages 40 and 156)
THE LANGUAGE OF DISCUSSION (pages 141−152)

33. JOANNA (for groups of 2–3 learners)

The following two letters have been found in a park, in one envelope. There are no dates or addresses on them. Try to work out the history of Joanna and P's relationship.

You might want to consider the following questions:

1. Where and in what circumstances did Joanna and P meet?
2. Do they know each other well?
3. Are they still in touch with each other?
4. What is the sequence of the letters?

Joanna, what <u>am</u> I going to do with you!
    My wife was upset by your first letter and would have been very upset by the second one. I love her. That's why I behaved so tediously correctly towards you. At all times.
    Look, I hope I'll see you in London. Until then, I wish you lots of luck and I hope you will find someone who knows more about women than I evidently do. But, Joanna, no more letters and no more contact of any kind, OK.

                                                  P

Dear Joanna,
    I was very pleased to get your letter. I'm glad you were pleased with mine. I had been meaning to get in touch before, but did have a very busy year. We seem both to have hesitated in a similar fashion ... I'm sorry you were often lonely and depressed while here; I suppose I suspected some sort of sadness, and am glad if I helped - even briefly - to cheer you up. I enjoyed that day and our chat too.
    You <u>didn't</u> drink too many Camparis and weren't drunk, or if you were, <u>you did</u> very well at appearing sober! And Cornwall ... I'd got the impression you must have some boyfriend there; I suppose I'm good at intuiting things sometimes, but I probably got it wrong?! You certainly told me not much more than that you were going there, and seemed a bit mysterious about it! I hope your job continues well. I can understand your feeling glad to be back in Poland. I've never had Polish bread - black maybe? - and home-made cottage cheese with fresh chives, but I hope it goes down well. My main acquaintance with Polish food and drink is a sip or two of Polish vodka and Krakow sausage, which seems OK. I also have a recipe for 'schab wieprzowy'; I assume schab means pig, and the rest is a chap or a place. I'll have to try it!
    No, I don't think it's too late to have a go at developing our friendship; we can try, can't we?
    Well, I'd better close; tell me about Poland, your job, yourself.
    Look after yourself.

                                            Love, P

Notes

1. If learners (who should be working in small groups) quickly come to the conclusion that the long letter preceded the short one, the teacher should point out that if P's wife was upset by the first letter, which in turn seems to have upset P himself, which letter was he pleased to receive in that case? That does *not* necessarily mean that the short letter is indeed the earlier one. The answer, however, might not be as transparent as it would appear initially.
2. As an optional follow-up activity, learners can be asked to
   (i) reconstruct at least one of Joanna's letters;
   (ii) reconstruct the conversation in which Cornwall was mentioned.

Language
See
ASKING ABOUT THE MEANING OF A WORD (pages 104 and 131)
EXPRESSING SUPPOSITION (pages 40 and 156)
THE LANGUAGE OF DISCUSSION (pages 141−152)

* * * * *

34. PUNISHMENT (for any number of learners)

In groups learners decide what kind of punishment (if indeed any) the following people deserve, irrespective of the existing laws.

---

1. A mother gives an overdose to her terminally ill daughter. Doctors say there is no hope for the girl's recovery.
2. A wife kills her unfaithful husband.
3. A drunken driver kills a child on a zebra crossing.
4. A drunken driver kills a child who suddenly runs into the middle of a road.
5. A driver kills a child who suddenly runs into the middle of a road.
6. A drug addict kills a drug trafficker.
7. A man kills his wife, who, according to him, is responsible for their son's suicidal death.
8. A teenager dares another one to climb to the top of a pylon. The boy does so and is electrocuted.

Note
This discussion can be conducted in the format of a pyramid discussion (see *Procedure* in Part One).

Language
The following vocabulary items may be needed in the discussion. (The definitions come from the *Oxford Advanced Learner's Dictionary of Current English*, third edition, 1974.)

euthanasia |ˌjuːθəˈneɪzɪə| — (bringing about of a) mercifully easy and painless death (for persons suffering from an incurable and painful disease).

homicide — killing of a human being.

manslaughter — act of killing a human being unlawfully but not wilfully.

murder — unlawful killing of a human being on purpose.

pylon |ˈpaɪlən| — tower (steel framework) for carrying overhead high-voltage electric cables.

Some useful phrases:

a cold-blooded murder

to kill somebody in cold blood

a crime of passion

extenuating circumstances

diminished responsibility

See also

STALLING FOR TIME (pages 32 and 154)

MAKING EVERYBODY ACTIVE (pages 69 and 151–152)

THE LANGUAGE OF DISCUSSION (pages 141–152)

* * * * *

35. LONELY HEARTS (for any number of learners)

Gill Littlewood, a bored married woman, decided to amuse herself by placing a lonely hearts advertisement in a popular newspaper.

> **Sensitive, quiet,** badly hurt in the past, completely unattached and alone, shy and reserved woman seeks an understanding man for genuine friendship and companionship. Box 453.

Gill received quite a few replies. She answered the most interesting and promising one. It came from Len Shade. Gill created a new identity for herself — an identity that would melt anybody's heart, let alone Len's, who was lonely and disillusioned himself. After a few months of fairly frequent meetings full of confidences and plans for the future, Gill grew tired and lost interest in her game. She withdrew in a callous and abrupt manner. Soon after, Len Shade committed suicide.

Procedure

1. Learners read (or listen to) the description of the situation.

2. They evaluate Gill's actions. Here are some of the points they might want to bring up:

- Len would have committed suicide anyway if he had been inclined that way;
- nothing can justify toying with other people's emotions;
- answering a lonely hearts advertisement means asking for trouble;
- right from the beginning Gill was perfectly aware of what she was up to.

3. Learners consider if the situation would have been in any way different, if an advertisement had been placed in good faith (e.g. by Len) and answered for fun (e.g. by Gill).
4. Learners consider if the situation would have been in any way different, if the advertisement had been placed for fun by a man and answered in good faith by a woman.
5. (optional) One learner is chosen to play Gill Littlewood. The class is divided into two groups of roughly the same size. One of them accuses Gill of a heartless cold-blooded deed, the other claims that nobody but Len himself can be blamed for his suicide. Gill can explain her point of view; she can also be questioned by other learners (e.g. regarding her motives). As opinions are assigned (see *Agree!*), learners might have to argue against their personal views.

Alternative procedure

1. The situation is presented to the learners but they are not told about Len's suicide.
2. Learners evaluate Gill's actions.
3. They are told about Len's suicide.
4. Learners decide whether the fact than Len committed suicide should change their opinion about Gill and what she did.

Language

When discussing what happened between Gill and Len, learners will need to refer to past unfulfilled conditions, e.g. If Gill hadn't placed that advertisement, Len wouldn't have committed suicide.

When discussing the problem in more general terms, learners may talk about cause and effect, e.g. If you place a lonely advertisement, you can expect something like this to happen.

BE CAREFUL:
The correct phrase is commit suicide.

See also

STALLING FOR TIME (pages 32 and 154)
MAKING EVERYBODY ACTIVE (pages 69 and 151—152)
THE LANGUAGE OF DISCUSSION (pages 141—152)

36. AGONY AUNT (2) (for any number of learners)

```
Dear Sandy,
     Peter and I are very much in love.  Unfortunately he is
unhappily married and has a four-year-old son.  Our life is
unbearable.  Peter says he will leave his wife if I ask him to.  I
love him but I don't know what to do.  Please help me.
                                              Ellen
```

Procedure
1. The learners individually decide what to tell Ellen. They need not write the actual letter.
2. The learners who have come to the same (or similar) decision are put in small groups. They are then told that their reply resulted in a tragedy. One of the people involved committed suicide. The groups have to decide to what extent the Agony Aunt was responsible for the tragedy.

Note
Depending on the decision the learners make in the first stage of the activity, the teacher decides who committed suicide. Here are some suggestions (they should not be disclosed to the learners):

Agony Aunt's suggestion	Consequences
Peter should leave his wife	Peter's wife commits suicide
Ellen should stop seeing Peter	Ellen stops seeing Peter; commits suicide soon after
Things should stay as they are	Peter's wife finds out, commits suicide, Peter stops seeing Ellen
Ellen should tell Peter to make a decision	Peter commits suicide
Agony Aunt gives an evasive answer (or does not answer the letter at all)	Ellen commits suicide

Language
When discussing what to tell Ellen, learners will need to talk about conditions that may be fulfilled in the future, e.g. *If Peter leaves his wife, she will be very unhappy.*

When discussing what happened after the Agony Aunt's reply, learners will need to refer to past unfulfilled conditions, e.g. *If Peter hadn't left his wife, she wouldn't have committed suicide.*

BE CAREFUL:
The correct phrase is commit suicide.

See also
AGONY AUNT (1) (page 99)
MAKING EVERYBODY ACTIVE (pages 69 and 151−152)
THE LANGUAGE OF DISCUSSION (pages 141−152)

37. ROBERT SLATER (for groups of 2−4 learners)

Margaret Danby married Charles Croft and became Margaret Croft. Charles Croft died. Margaret married Robert Slater and called herself Margaret Croft-Slater.

Margaret Croft-Slater died a month ago. Her second husband, Robert Slater, is old and definitely unable to cope on his own. None of the Crofts is willing to look after him. There are no Slaters left. A home for the elderly is out of the question.

In small groups discuss the situation and decide who *should* look after Robert Slater.

The Croft family tree

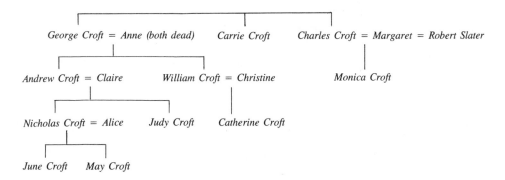

Monica Croft.   Before Monica became independent, she was treated very badly by Robert Slater, her stepfather.

Carrie Croft.   An eccentric old maid.

Andrew and Claire Croft.   Distinguished scientists, engaged in very important experiments.

Nicholas and Alice Croft.   Alice is expecting a baby. They have two young children, June (aged two) and May (aged one).

Judy Croft, eighteen.   She is studying for a very difficult entrance exam to university.

William and Christine Croft.   Three years ago they asked Robert Slater to use his connections to help their daughter, Catherine, then seventeen, to get a very good job. He refused.

Catherine Croft, now twenty.   Her parents have strictly forbidden her to look after Robert Slater.

Language

The family relationships between Robert Slater and all the Crofts (except for Monica, his *stepdaughter*) are very remote and by marriage only. Margaret, his late wife, was Carrie's *sister-in-law*, Andrew and William's *aunt* and Nicholas, Judy and Catherine's *great-aunt*. That made Andrew and William her *nephews*, Claire and Christine her *nieces*, Nicholas her *great-nephew* and Alice, Judy and Catherine her *great-nieces*.

See also

ASKING FOR ADVICE (with a change of personal pronouns) (pages 78 and 127–128)
OFFERING ADVICE (with a change of personal pronouns) (pages 78 and 127)
STALLING FOR TIME (pages 32 and 154)
THE LANGUAGE OF DISCUSSION (pages 141–152)

*****

38.   THINK OF A STORY (for groups of 2–3 learners)

Procedure

1. Pairs or threes of learners are given 3–6 phrases or sentences, which they are to incorporate into narratives of their own. All groups get the same sets so that their stories can then be compared.
2. After a few minutes learners present their stories, while others challenge them.
3. Learners vote for the best story.

Example

A woman is doing her shopping.
A woman is sleeping.
A man is standing in front of an empty refrigerator.

Possible answers

1. The husband discovers there is no food in the house and tells off his wife. She goes shopping. After that she has a nap.
2. A woman is sleeping. She dreams that there is no food in the house and she has to go shopping, which she does not like very much.
3. A man discovers there is no food in the refrigerator. He is very angry with his housekeeper, who is sleeping as usual instead of doing the shopping.

Alternative procedures

1. Learners are given a list of about ten phrases or sentences and they are to use as many of them as possible. They are allowed to leave out the ones they they cannot find a place for.
2. Learners prepare their stories individually in writing as their homework assignment. The stories are then read out and challenged in class.
3. Learners prepare sets of phrases or sentences for each other. Any of the suggested procedures are suitable.

Notes

1. When preparing the narratives, learners can add anything they like in between the given phrases and sentences.
2. Only the sentences in quotation marks have to be quoted exactly. The other phrases and sentences can appear in any form that is justified by the narratives.

3. Instead of sentences, learners can be given pictures. Any of the above procedures can be followed.
4. The teacher can decide whether the sequence of the sentences or pictures has to remain unchanged.

Sets of phrases and sentences for learners to work on

I

'Pierre, I know it's none of my business but ... what *am* I doing here?'
'Not even with lemon?'
'Come in the morning and I'll have another look at you.'
'Hold it.'
'I like your hat.'

II

A small doll.
An inkpot.
A tropical forest.
A silver tea service.
A bus ticket.

III

A young man is playing a game of Patience.
A child is playing a saxophone.
A nurse is smoking a cigar.
A middle-aged man is talking to a group of children in bathing suits.

IV

A book of fairy tales.
An empty picture frame.
A magnifying glass.
A crumpled banknote.
A giant panda.

V

'Just as long as it's quick.'
'Is it David himself?'
'Fabulous,' he repeated softly.
'Athens, Georgia.'

VI

'What are you doing? Planning a ... No, you aren't, are you?'
'Speaking.'
'Well,' I said, 'and what did he have to say today?'
'I hate champagne.'

VII

An old-fashioned key.
A mug of coffee.
An English–Bulgarian phrase book.
A lighthouse.
An empty ballroom.

VIII
A dog is sitting beside a trombone.
Two pigeons are flying over a park bench.
An elegant, elderly woman is using a computer.
A teenage boy is talking to a girl in an old-fashioned dress.
A girl is sitting at her desk thinking hard.
IX
'Jump!'
There was disbelief in her voice.
A glass bowl with a goldfish in it.
A typewriter.
A clean blackboard.
'I'm sorry if I've interrupted.'
We walked in silence.
Then suddenly the bell rang and I froze.
'Read me the story in that case.'
I needed a new toothbrush.
X
A policeman is getting out of a police-car.
A young couple are looking at a pram with a dog in it.
A slice of lemon.
A hair dryer.
A watermelon.
A flowerpot with a geranium in it.
An empty room. There is only a pile of books on the floor.
'It's upstairs. I can run up and get it.'
'Not my sister. A friend.'
Three coins.

Language
See
ASKING FOR ADVICE (pages 78 and 127–128)
OFFERING ADVICE (pages 78 and 127)
OFFERING HELP (page 134)
ACCEPTING AN OFFER OF HELP (page 134)
REJECTING AN OFFER OF HELP (page 134)
EXPRESSING INABILITY TO HELP (page 135)
RESPONDING TO THE ABOVE (page 135)
THE LANGUAGE OF DISCUSSION (pages 141–152)

39. AGREE! (for any number of learners)

1. A controversial motion is put forward.
2. Learners draw lots which will determine whether they are in favour or against the motion. They think of the arguments they can use.
3. A discussion follows.

Notes

1. There should be roughly the same number of lots marked for and against the proposal.
2. Since views are drawn, learners might find themselves arguing against their personal opinions. This can be a very stimulating factor, which will enhance the discussion.

Alternative procedure

A panel discussion is organised with four or six learners taking part in it. Half of them are for the issue in question and half are against. (Which view the learners are to support is established in a draw.) The discussion is followed by a vote, which will indicate whose arguments the audience (that is the rest of the learners) found most convincing.

Some controversial subjects that can be discussed:

1. All laws should be abolished and individuals should be responsible for their own actions.

2.

> HARMONICS will lift all stress from your life. HARMONICS retrains you to be a member of the HARMONIC Community. Come on our Introductory Course Weekend and we will guarantee that you will never leave us, our solutions to all your problems are so complete! Box 257.

Agencies like HARMONICS should be banned.
3. Marriages should be arranged by parents.
4. Male prostitution should be legalised.
5. Education should not be obligatory.
6. The minimum age for marrying should be twenty-five.
7. Cleaners should earn more than engineers.
8. Two years' military or community service should be compulsory for men and women.
9. Children should not be given any pocket money.
10. School is the best time of one's life.
11. Beauty contests are degrading to women.
12. Nudism should be banned.
13. Since smokers frequently fall ill, they should be paid less.
14. Couples with children under eighteen should never be granted divorces.

15. Private health service is socially unjust.
16. There is nothing wrong with picking one's teeth in public.
17. Telephones constitute an invasion of privacy.

Language
BE CAREFUL:
The stress in 'obligatory' falls on the second syllable.

See also
MAKING EVERYBODY ACTIVE (pages 69 and 151−152)
THE LANGUAGE OF DISCUSSION (pages 141−152)

Part Three

The Language

INTRODUCTION — HOW TO USE PART THREE

The progression

Part Three contains all the language used in this book. The language is arranged in a progressive order rather like the way a conversation or friendship develops, starting with greetings and explorations, entering into light conversation, then discussion, then more emotional conversation. To look up a particular function, see the contents pages at the beginning of this book.

For the teacher

As well as being used for reference and as a resource, it can be used for self-access, the teacher reading through it to remind herself of the language used.

For the learner

The learner can use the language for revision or pre-preparation. The most active method is for the learners, in pairs, to talk through, using each of the functions in turn, *inserting* their own *content* into the language used.

The layout

These pages are laid out, wherever possible, with the 'openers' in the left-hand column and the 'responses' in the right-hand column. To open a conversation or a new subject in conversation 'openers' are used, and the appropriate responses are next to those 'openers' in the right hand column.

Where language can be used as openers or responses, arrows indicate the possible directions of the conversation.

OPENERS

GREETINGS

Good morning.
Good afternoon.
Good evening.
Morning.
Hello.

How are you [getting along / keeping / doing / Ø] [nowadays / these days / Ø] ?

Hello. How [are things / is life treating you] ?

INTRODUCING ONESELF

I don't think we've met before .
May I introduce myself?

My name is ... / I'm ... [from .... / ...'s wife/husband] .

RESPONSES

RESPONDING TO GREETINGS

[Very well / Fine] [thank you / thanks] . And you?

Can't complain...
Not too well, I'm afraid....

RESPONDING TO SOMEONE INTRODUCING THEMSELVES

How do you do?
Pleased to meet you.
I've been wanting to meet you for some time now.

I've heard [a lot / such a lot / so much] about you.

INTRODUCING SOMEONE

May I introduce | you to / Ø | ...? This is ....

This is ... This is ....
John... Mary.
John, I'd like you to meet...

Have you two met before? This is... This is ....

Do you know...? This is ....

ASKING YES/NO QUESTIONS ABOUT INTERESTS AND LIKES

Are you | interested in / keen on | ....?

Do you | like / enjoy | ....?

Do you take much interest in ....?

RESPONDING TO BEING INTRODUCED TO SOMEONE

We've already met, actually.
Yes, as a matter of fact we have.

No, I don't think | I do / so | actually.

ANSWERING YES/NO QUESTIONS ABOUT INTERESTS AND LIKES

Yes, | as a matter of fact / actually / Ø | | I do / I am | .

Yes, very much | indeed / Ø | .

| Oh, / Ø | | I love ... / yes, very much | !

OPENERS

Have you | got / Ø | any favourite … ?

ASKING WH- QUESTIONS ABOUT INTERESTS AND LIKES

What | are / is | your favourite … ?

RESPONSES

Well, | as a matter of fact / actually / frankly speaking / frankly / to be honest / Ø

…

I prefer / I am rather more interested in / I am more into

Oh, I don't know.

No, | not really / I'm not particularly keen on … / I don't particularly enjoy …

No, I'm afraid | I'm not / I don't

ANSWERING WH- QUESTIONS ABOUT INTERESTS AND LIKES

I am | rather / quite / Ø | interested in / keen on

…

I | rather / quite / Ø | like / enjoy | . . .

Oh, / Ø | I love . . . .

Oh, / Ø | I like . . . | very much / Ø | .

What | kind / Ø | of . . . do you | like best / like / enjoy most / enjoy | ?

What | kind of / Ø | . . . are you | interested in / keen on | ?

EXPRESSING AGREEMENT WITH SOMEBODY'S LIKES

So | do I, / am I, | as a matter of fact / actually / Ø | .

I do / I am | too, | as a matter of fact / actually / Ø | .

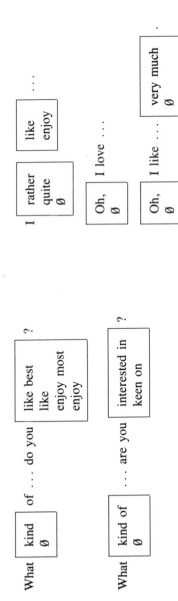
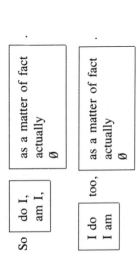

RESPONSES

OPENERS

EXPRESSING AGREEMENT WITH SOMEBODY'S DISLIKES

Neither	do I,	as a matter of fact
Nor	am I,	actually
		Ø

.

I don't	either,	as a matter of fact
I am not		actually
		Ø

.

ASKING ABOUT PLANS

Have you got any plans?
Have you made any plans yet?
Have you got anything in mind?
What are you planning to do?

RESPONDING — BEING EVASIVE

No, not really. | What | about you?
                  | How |

Well	, nothing	special
No		in particular
Oh		worth talking about
		worth mentioning

.

| What | about you?
| How |

I don't know yet. | What | about you?
                    | How |

ASKING ABOUT PLANS

What are you doing ....?
Are you doing anything ....?
Have you got anything planned for ....?
Have you made any plans for ....?

RESPONDING — NOTHING DEFINITE

I don't know yet. Why?

No, / Ø	nothing / special in particular

. Why?

Well, I was thinking of ....

RESPONDING — DEFINITE PLANS

Yes, / Ø	I'm ....

Well, | as a matter of fact / actually / frankly speaking / Ø | I've arranged to / I'm | ...

OFFERING ADVICE

If I were you, I'd ....
Personally, I'd advise you to ....
I think you should ....

Well, you could | always / Ø | ...

ASKING FOR ADVICE

What do you | think / suggest | we should do / should be done | ?

What should we do | in that case / then / Ø | ?

RESPONSES

OPENERS

What are we going to do about | all this / this business | ?

What do you | think / suggest | ?

| I should do / should be done | ?

What | shall / should | I do | in that case / then / Ø | ?

What am I to do | in that case / then / Ø | ?

What would you do in my position?

MAKING REQUESTS

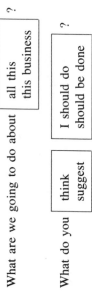

| Can / Could / Will / Would | you . . . ., please?

Would you mind . . . ., please?
Would you mind if . . . .?

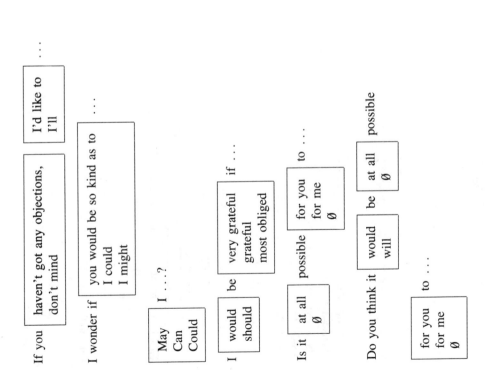

If you | haven't got any objections, / don't mind | I'd like to / I'll | . . .

I wonder if | you would be so kind as to / I could / I might | . . .

May / Can / Could | I . . .?

I | would / should | be | very grateful / grateful / most obliged | if . . .

Is it | at all / Ø | possible | for you / for me / Ø | to . . .

Do you think it | would / will | be | at all / Ø | possible | for you / for me / Ø | to . . .

RESPONSES

RESPONDING TO COMPLIMENTS

Thank you.

OPENERS

Do you think | you / I | could ....?

Would you | kindly / Ø | ..., please?

All of the above can be preceded by:
Excuse me, but ....
The above can also be used for:
ASKING FOR HELP
LEADING TO A QUESTION

PAYING COMPLIMENTS

What a | beautiful / charming / fantastic | ... | you've got / Ø | .

This is a | great / lovely / marvellous | ..., isn't it?

Isn't that a | pretty / smashing / super | ...!

I like your ....

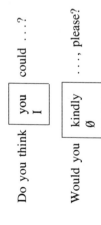
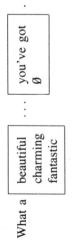

ASKING ABOUT THE MEANING OF A WORD

Do you know
Have you any idea   what ....   [can mean   ?]
Can you tell me   [means   ]

I wonder what ....   [can mean   .]
                     [means   ]

What is the meaning of ....?
What is ...?

What   [can]   ... mean?
       [does]

Do you know
Have you any idea   what the meaning of .... is?
Can you tell me

DEFINING

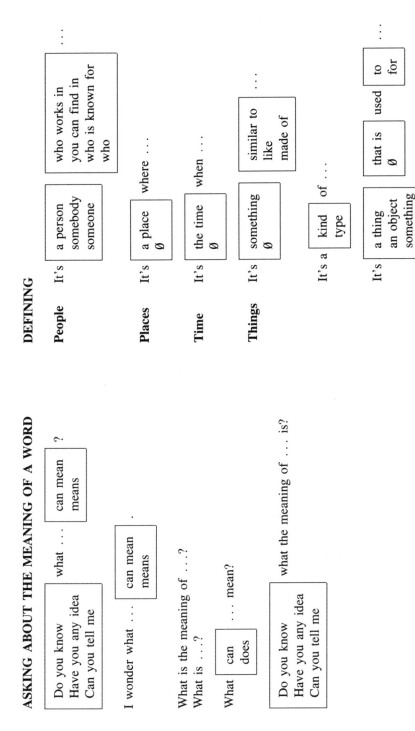

People   It's   [a person   ]   who works in ...
                    [somebody   ]   you can find in ...
                    [someone   ]   who is known for ...
                                     who ...

Places   It's   [a place]   where ....
                    [Ø   ]

Time   It's   [the time]   when ....
                    [Ø   ]

Things   It's   [something]   similar to ...
                    [Ø   ]   like ...
                                    made of ...

             It's a   [kind]   of ....
                      [type]

             It's   [a thing   ]   that is ...   [used   to ...]
                    [an object]   Ø   [for ...]
                    [something   ]

             People use it   [to ....]
                             [for ....]

OPENERS

RESPONSES

Actions It's what | people / you | do when ....

It's | a way of / like / similar to | ...

It's a movement

like ....
like this (accompanied by a gesture or movement)

Qualitites It's | similar to / the opposite of / the same as | ...

Other It's something to do with ....

It's a general | word / term | for ....

TALKING ABUT THE WEATHER

Have you	heard	the weather forecast	for	today?
	seen		Ø	
	read			

It looks like rain, doesn't it?
Looks a bit like rain, doesn't it?
I suppose it'll clear up later.
Isn't it awful today?

What a	chilly	day	!
	freezing	morning	
	lovely	afternoon	
	marvellous	evening	
	rainy	night	
	terrible		

It's very	foggy	today, isn't it?
	hot	
	mild	
	sunny	
	wet	

It's been very	cold	this week	, hasn't it?
	nice	this summer	
	warm	these past few days	
	windy		

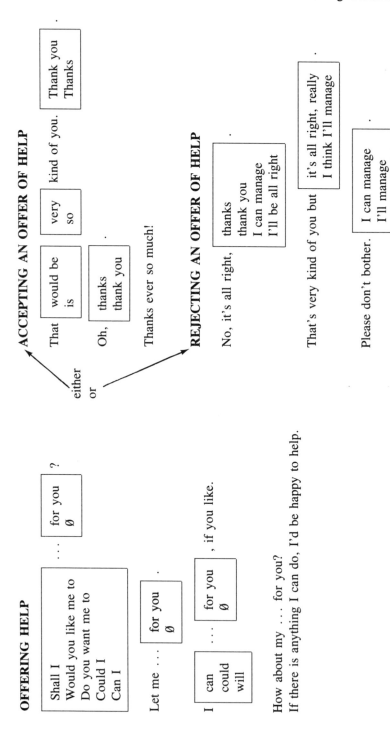

OPENERS

OFFERING HELP

Shall I
Would you like me to
Do you want me to
Could I
Can I

... | for you / Ø | ?

Let me ... | for you / Ø | .

I | can / could / will | ... | for you / Ø | , if you like.

How about my ... for you?
If there is anything I can do, I'd be happy to help.

RESPONSES

either → ACCEPTING AN OFFER OF HELP
or → REJECTING AN OFFER OF HELP

ACCEPTING AN OFFER OF HELP

That | would be / is | very / so | kind of you. | Thank you / Thanks | .

Oh, | thanks / thank you | .

Thanks ever so much!

REJECTING AN OFFER OF HELP

No, it's all right, | thanks / thank you / I can manage / I'll be all right | .

That's very kind of you but | it's all right, really / I think I'll manage | .

Please don't bother. | I can manage / I'll manage / I'll be all right / I'm all right | .

EXPRESSING INABILITY TO HELP ⟶ RESPONDING

I'd really like to help but ....
I wish I could help you but ....
I'm afraid I can't ....

Please don't worry,	I can	manage	somehow	.
Never mind,	I'll		Ø	
Not to worry.				
That's all right,				

APOLOGISING (before)

I'm afraid I've got to ...
I hope I'm not disturbing you ....

Sorry to bother you | just now
| with something like this | ...

Excuse me ....
The above can also be used for
STARTING A CONVERSATION

APOLOGISING (after)

I can't tell you how sorry I am.

Sorry to have | kept you waiting.
| bothered you.

I'm	terribly	sorry	you should take it that way
	ever so		. I just don't know what to do
	very		, I didn't realise
	so		about all this
	Ø		
.

I beg your pardon.
Do accept my apologies.

RESPONDING TO APOLOGIES

| That's | quite | all right. |
| It's | Ø | |

| It's | my fault | entirely | . |
| Ø | | Ø | |

OPENERS

SERVING A CLIENT

| Can |
| May |

I help you, | madam |
| sir | ?

What can I do for you, | madam |
| sir | ?

RESPONDING TO CLIENTS

SCRIBA employee:

We'll certainly do our best, | madam |
| sir | .

Can you give me the details, please?

Can you show me the advertisement

| you'd like |
| you wish | to answer?

What would you like to say in

| your |
| the | | advertisement |
| letter |
| application | ?

RESPONSES

CLIENT'S OPENING WORDS

SCRIBA client:

I wonder if you could help me:

| I'd like to apply for a job. |
| I'd like to send a letter. |
| I'd like to place an advertisement. |

CLIENT ENQUIRY

SCRIBA client: (provides the details and then asks)

What else do you think I should

| include in my application |
| include in my advertisement |
| write in my letter | ?

GETTING DETAILS FROM CLIENTS

SCRIBA employee:

Can you think of any other | details / pieces of information | ?

Is there anything else | we / I | can do for you, | madam / sir | ?

INTERVIEWING – QUESTIONS

When talking to a prospective employee:

What | kind / type | of | post / job / employment / position | would you be / are you | interested in / looking for | ?

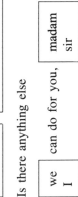
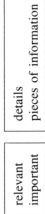

What are your qualifications?

Have you | got / Ø | any relevant | experience / training | ?

BEING INTERVIEWED – ANSWERS

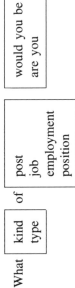

Well, what I'm | looking for / interested in | is . . . .

I've got the right background for the job.

OPENERS

Can
Do

you | speak any foreign languages / type / drive / take shorthand | ?

Have you got a driving licence?
What foreign languages do you speak?

When would you | like / be willing | to start?

When | could / can | you start?

When | would / will / could / can | you be available for an interview?

BEING INTERVIEWED – QUESTIONS

When talking to a prospective employer:
What are your requirements?

RESPONSES

My | French / typing / shorthand | is pretty good.

I'm hoping to start as soon as possible.

I could start next | week / month | .

INTERVIEWING – ANSWERS

The sort of person we're | looking for / interested in | is ...

What | qualifications / kind of experience / type of training | would you | expect / be expected / be looking for | ?   The background we're looking for is ....

What | kind of / Ø | conditions are you offering?

For this job you need | to be / to have | ...

What should the | candidates / applicants | be | like / able to do / proficient in | ?

When | would you want / would you like / do you want | the | candidate / applicant | to start?

See also
TALKING ON THE TELEPHONE

TALKING ON THE TELEPHONE

CALLER SPEAKS FIRST

| Could / Can | I speak | with / to | ..., please?

I wonder if I could speak | with / to | ..., please.

ANSWERER RESPONDS

I'm afraid | she / he | is | not in / out | at the moment / just now / Ø | .

Could I take a message?

Would you like | to leave a message / John to call you back | ?

RESPONSES

ACCEPTING AN INVITATION

That sounds very | nice / interesting | indeed.

That's very | kind / nice | of you. | Thank you / Thanks |.

Yes, | I'd love to / I'd love that / that would be fun / that would be interesting / let's / I'd be delighted |.

Yes, that sounds | fantastic / fun / great / lovely / marvellous / wonderful |.

OPENERS

EXTENDING AN INVITATION

I was wondering if you'd | like to / care to / be interested in | ...

| How / Ø | would you like to ...?

Would you care to ...?

Would you be interested in ...?

| How / What | about ...?

REFUSING AN INVITATION

[Thank you / Thanks] but I don't really think I can. You see ....

I can't, I'm afraid. Some other time, perhaps.

I'm [so / Ø] sorry but I can't.

That's very [kind / nice] of you but I'm afraid ....

[Thank you / Thanks / I wish I could / It's very kind of you to invite me] but I'm afraid ....

GIVING CLARIFICATION

Well, [Ø] [what / all] I'm [trying to say / saying] is that ....

Well, [Ø] what I mean is ....

ASKING FOR CLARIFICATION

Could you explain what you mean [by this / Ø], please? I'm not quite with you.

What do you mean?

RESPONSES

Well, / Ø ┃ the point is ....

OPENERS

I'm sorry but / I'm afraid / Ø ┃ I don't ┃ quite / really / Ø ┃ understand what you

are trying to say / mean by this / are getting at / are driving at .

I'm sorry but / I'm afraid / Ø ┃ I'm not clear about ....

I'm not ┃ quite / Ø ┃ sure I ┃ understand that / follow you / know that you mean .

I'm afraid I can't even begin to understand what you are trying to say.

ASKING FOR OPINIONS

What do you think ┃ about / of ┃ ... ?

EXPRESSING OPINIONS

Personally / Frankly / Ø ┃ I think that ....

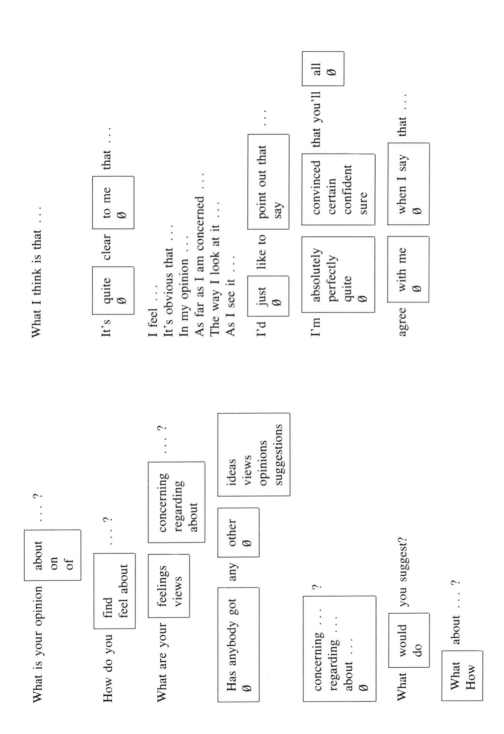

What I think is that ....

It's | quite / Ø | clear | to me / Ø | that ....

I feel ....
It's obvious that ....
In my opinion ....
As far as I am concerned ....
The way I look at it ....
As I see it ....

I'd | just / Ø | like to | point out that / say | ....

I'm | absolutely / perfectly / quite / Ø | convinced / certain / confident / sure | that you'll | all / Ø |

agree | with me / Ø | when I say / Ø | that ....

What is your opinion | about / on / of | .... ?

How do you | find / feel about | .... ?

What are your | feelings / views | concerning / regarding / about | .... ?

Has anybody got | any | other / Ø | ideas / views / opinions / suggestions

concerning .... / regarding .... / about .... / Ø | ? | would / do | you suggest?

What | would / do | you suggest?

What / How | about .... ?

RESPONSES

OPENERS

What would you say | about / to | ... ?

How does the idea of ... appeal to you?

| Would / Will | it be a good idea | if / to | ... ?

| Will / Won't / Would / Wouldn't / Do / Don't | you agree that ... ?

Except for 'What do you suggest?' the above can also be used for:
EXPRESSING OPINIONS
EXPRESSING SUGGESTIONS

INTRODUCING A POINT

I'm | sure / convinced / absolutely certain | that ....

EXPRESSING AGREEMENT

I couldn't agree more.
I agree entirely.

I fully agree with | what you have just said / your comment | .

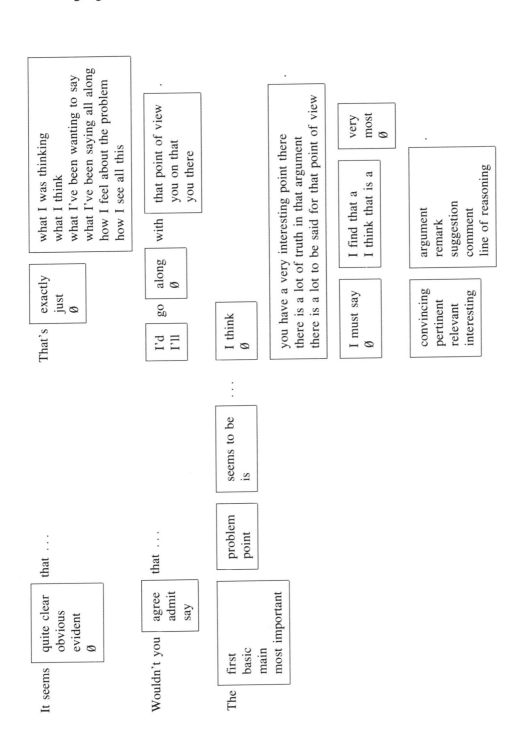

RESPONSES

INTRODUCING AN OPPOSITE POINT

I | take / see | you point but ....

| Possibly, / True, / Yes, | but

on the other hand ....
if you look at this from a different point of view ....
looking at this from another point of view ....

EXPRESSING ALTERNATIVE SUGGESTIONS

Don't you think | I / you / he / she / it / we | 'd better ....?

OPENERS

EXPRESSING SUGGESTIONS

Don't you think | I / you / he / she / it / we / they | could / should | ....?

Don't you think it would be [a good / a sensible / an] idea to ....?

One way out would be to ....

Wouldn't it be possible for [me / you / him / her / it / us / them] to ....?

[thought of / thought about / considered] ....?

Have you [ever / Ø] ....?

Why don't [I / you / we / they] ...?

Why doesn't [he / she / it] ...?

Can't / Couldn't [I / you / he / she / it / we / they] .... instead?

I must say [I'd rather .... / Ø]

Wouldn't it be better [if / to] ....?

Don't you think it would be better [if / to] ....?

EXPRESSING TENTATIVE AGREEMENT

That [certainly / Ø] [sounds / seems] like a good idea.

That's [certainly / definitely / Ø] [a possibility / something to consider / something worth consideration].

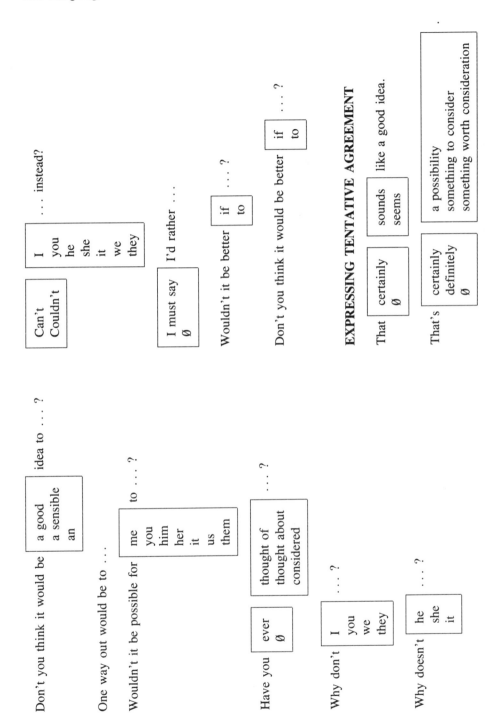

RESPONSES

EXPRESSING DISAGREEMENT IN A DISCUSSION

Wouldn't it be rather risky to .... ?
You haven't convinced me that ....
Isn't that out of the question?
I can't accept that.
Do you expect me to believe that?
No way.
What an absurd idea!

OPENERS

Why not .... ?
Let's ...

Let	me
	him
	her
	it
	them

...

I thought	I	would
Ø	you	could
	he
	she
	it
	we
	they

... ?

Can	I
Can't	you
Could	he
Couldn't	she
	it
	we
	they

.... ?

| I | 'd better .... |

I don't suppose | you / she / they | would | like to / fancy / ∅ | ... ?

All of the above can be preceded by:

You | might / may | not agree with me but ...

See also
ASKING FOR OPINIONS

EXPRESSING DOUBT

I | take / see | your point but ....

I see what you mean but ...
I agree with you on the whole but ...

Perhaps / Possibly / Yes | , but ....

Oh, but don't you | think / see | that .... ?

DEALING WITH DOUBTS AND OBJECTIONS

I can assure you that ....
You needn't worry about ....
Look at it in another way ....

This may seem | impossible / improbable | to you but ...

RESPONSES

EXPRESSING DISAGREEMENT

I'm rather worried about what you said ...
I honestly don't see why ...
I don't think there is any need to ...

I'm not sure
I don't think

I quite agree
I'll go along with you on that
I'll go along with you there
it would be advisable to ...
I can accept that suggestion

You see ....

I wouldn't agree.
I don't agree at all.
You can't really mean that.
You don't mean that, do you?
You don't seem to realise that ...
Surely you realise that ...
Are you really trying to say that ....?

You don't seem to understand what I'm | driving at / trying to say / saying |

I'm afraid | Ø | that's | quite / Ø | out of the question.

OPENERS

That's all very well but ...

That's true | I suppose / Ø | but ...

That's an interesting | point of view / comment / remark | but ...

That's easier said than done. You see ...
Well, you have a point there but ...
It's all very well for you to say that but ...

It | all / Ø | sounds | quite / most / very / Ø | interesting / convincing | but ...

Might it not also be true that ....?
Isn't it just possible that ...?
Can we be sure that ....?
What will happen if ....?
Yes, but you don't seem to realise that ...

The above can also be used for:
POLITE DISAGREEMENT

Yes, but [on the other hand / you can't deny that / you've got to remember that / don't forget that] ....

It's not as easy as all that. You see ....

Well, [actually / to be quite honest / I'm afraid that] ....

Oh, do you really think so?

Most of the above can be preceded by:
That's a very good idea but ....

INTERRUPTING

By the way ....
Sorry to interrupt but ....

That's [all / Ø] very interesting but ....

Excuse me but [that reminds me ....]
Ø

I'm afraid / I'm sorry but [I've got / I have] to interrupt you [here / Ø] .

See also
EXPRESSING INDECISION

EXPRESSING INDECISION

Oh, I don't know ....

I'm not [really / Ø] sure.

The above can also be used for:
POLITE DISAGREEMENT

MAKING EVERYBODY ACTIVE

What do you think, Mrs Davis?

[Don't / Do] you agree, Miss Pullen?

I don't know what Mr Millington thinks but ....
You're very quiet, Mrs Patterson.

You haven't said [anything / much] so far, Dr Loft.

OPENERS

Let's hear what Mrs Patterson | thinks / says / has to say | .

RESPONSES

I'm afraid / I'm sorry but | I've got / I have | something | important / Ø |

to tell you.

EXPRESSING EXASPERATION at not being listened to

Why doesn't / Won't | anybody | ever / Ø |

listen to me / take any notice of what I'm saying ?

Why | can't / won't | you listen to me | for once / Ø | ?

BRINGING A DISCUSSION BACK TO THE POINT

Please come to the point ....
The whole point is that ....
Could you stick to the point, please?
Perhaps we could get back to the main point.
That's off the point.

That's | all / Ø | very interesting but I don't think it's really

to the point.

I'm afraid / Ø | that's not the point / you've missed the point .

Can we leave that and | get / go | back to .... .

We seem to be talking at cross-purposes.

This isn't | very / Ø | relevant, | is it / Ø | ?

LODGING COMPLAINTS politely

I'm very	sorry	to have to say this	but . . . .
I'm ever so		to say this	
I'm		to mention this	
Ø		to bring this up	

	to have to say this	but . . . .
I hate	to say this	
I don't like	to mention this	
	to bring this up	

I hope you don't mind my	saying this	but . . . .
I hate	mentioning this	
I don't like	bringing this up	
Forgive me for		

All of the above opening phrases can be followed by a statement of fact and a request, e.g.

'Forgive me for saying this but I have an awful headache, so could you please turn down the radio?'

or by request only, e.g.

'Forgive me for saying this but could you please turn down the radio?'

Those phrases can also be used for making very polite requests (with no implication of complaining).

EXPRESSING WORRY

That's all very well, but . . . .
Can we be sure that . . . .
What will happen if . . . .
All this sounds like a real bargain and that's precisely what makes it so suspicious.
That's all true, I suppose, but can we really . . . .
I'm not sure we should . . . .

REASSURING SOMEBODY

You needn't worry about	anything	.
	a thing	

This may seem	impossible	but there'll be no . . . .
	strange to you	

CALMING SOMEBODY DOWN

Don't get	upset	.
	impatient	
	angry	

Calm down. There is no need to get	so	upset
	Ø	impatient
		angry

OPENERS

LODGING COMPLAINTS in a straightforward way

I've come to complain about .... (*politely*)
I've just about had enough of this! (*bluntly*)

Why can't you .... | once and for all | ?
                   | Ø |

| Why should I have to |
| I really can't | put up with this any more! |
| I won't |
| I don't see why I should |

BE CAREFUL:
Learners should be cautious of giving unintended offence by making blunt complaints.

ASKING TO ASK QUESTIONS

I wonder if you | can |
                | could |
                | would be so kind as to |

spare me a minute or two and answer a few questions.

I'd be interested to know why ....

RESPONSES

Well, we don't want to | make | any rash decisions, do we?
                       | take |

EXPRESSING ENTHUSIASM FOR AN IDEA

Well, all this certainly sounds like a marvellous idea, wouldn't you say so, dear?

That offer is definitely worth considering.

Surely it wouldn't be wise to miss an opportunity like this!

STALLING FOR TIME

Well, | let me see | ...
      | let's see |
      | let me think |
      | now |
      | how shall I put it |
      | how can I phrase this |
      | Ø |

I'm interested why . . .
I'd like to know why . . . .

BE CAREFUL:
Native English speakers almost never say 'I have a question'.

REFUSING TO ANSWER A QUESTION

If you don't mind I think I'm afraid	I'd rather not	say that answer that question tell you that discuss that subject

I'd prefer not to	say that answer that question tell you that discuss that subject

JOURNALISTS' QUESTIONS

These are some of the questions that the journalists can ask:

Why did you place this advertisement?
Why are you looking for . . . ?
Is . . . important for you? Why?
What will you do if you are not successful?

Each of the above questions can be preceded by the following phrases. This will make the questions more polite.

OPENERS

LEADING TO A QUESTION

I hope you don't mind my asking, but . . .

I wonder if | you'd allow me to | ask a few
             | I could |

| simple | questions . . . .
| ∅ |

EXPRESSING SUPPOSITION

I expect . . . .
I wouldn't be surprised if . . . .
I suppose . . . .
I don't suppose . . . .
What this probably means is . . . .
That might mean that . . . .
I don't know, but . . . .

References

Abbot, G., 1981, 'Encouraging communication in English: a paradox', *English Language Teaching Journal*, 35(3).

Alatis, J. E., 1976, 'The urge to communicate vs. resistance to learning in English as a second language', *English Language Teaching Journal*, 30(4).

Alexander, L. G., 1967, *Question and Answer*, Harlow: Longman.

Billows, F. L., 1961, *The Techniques of Language Learning*, Harlow: Longman.

Brumfit, C., 1981, 'Accuracy and fluency', *Practical English Teaching*, 1(3).

Brumfit, C., 1984, *Communicative Methodology in Language Teaching*, Cambridge: Cambridge University Press.

Finocchiaro, M. and Brumfit, C., 1983, *The Functional—Notional Approach: From Theory to Practice*, London: Oxford University Press.

Jones, K., 1981, 'Who's who, who sits where', *The Times Educational Supplement*, 14 August.

Jones, K., 1982, *Simulations in Language Teaching*, Cambridge: Cambridge University Press.

Livingstone, C., 1983, *Role Play in Language Learning*, Harlow: Longman.

McDonough, S. H., 1981, *Psychology in Foreign Language Teaching*, London: George Allen and Unwin.

Morrow, K., 1981, 'Principles of communicative methodology', in Johnson, K. and Morrow, K. (eds), *Communication in the Classroom*, Harlow: Longman.

Rivers, W. and Temperley, M., 1978, *A Practical Guide to the Teaching of English as a Second or Foreign Language*, New York: Oxford University Press.

Rixon, S., 1979, 'The "information gap" and the "opinion gap" — ensuring that communication games are communicative', *English Language Teaching Journal*, 33(2).

Willis, J., 1983, 'Chaos or control in the communicative classroom?', *Practical English Teaching*, 4(1).

Indexes

NUMBER OF PARTICIPANTS

Since in many cases the number of learners taking part in an activity is flexible, the same title may appear under several headings. (See *Emergency Role-Cards* in Part One.)